TOGETHER

Life in a Dorset Village

Rita Cruise O'Brien

For Donal and Arthur
great friends who loved the village
in memorium

Contents

Preface and acknowledgements   7

Prologue – Four people   9

Introduction to Owermoigne   12

Chapter One

From the earliest times to the estate and village   35

Chapter Two

Victorian Charity to World War Two   59

Chapter Three

Wartime Memories and After   92

Chapter Four

People at the Court   116

Chapter Five

Farmers, Plantsmen, Caravans: The Village Economy   128

Chapter Six

The Church   152

Chapter Seven

Newcomers and the Growth of the Village   166

Chapter Eight

Politics and the Parish Council   181

Chapter Nine

The Village Hall and Social Life   192

Chapter Ten

Dispute and Peace Restored   220

Chapter Eleven

Holworth People   227

Epilogue

The village in the early winter of 2014   237

Preface and acknowledgements

This is a historical and social portrait of Owermoigne, a small village a few miles from the coast on the main road between Dorchester and Wareham. The book has been some years in the making. I wish to thank the people of Owermoigne, Holworth and the surrounding area for being patient and waiting for published results. I have had a home in the village for sixteen years. It is a pleasant and friendly place to live, very welcoming and very sociable. All but a few people were happy to tell me about their lives both before and since they have lived in the village. For the contemporary social portrait, I interviewed more than seventy people. And I was able to see the village through a very bitter dispute in 2009-10 and out the other side, a gift for an observer.

Several people have had a large input in helping me complete my task. First among these is Martin Cree, the owner of Moignes Court, the estate in the village, who had often thought himself of writing a book on Owermoigne. He provided a great deal of information about his family and the history of the village in many conversations and looked carefully at early drafts. Alan Hodge, an excellent photographer, gave me many of his photographs which here accompany the text. Roger Holehouse, who lives in Whitcombe, first came to my attention in 2013 with his spirited map of the area from sources in The Domesday Book. He has done all the maps for the book expertly and graciously. As an accomplished local historian, he also corrected many misapprehensions from the early historical period. My sister-in-law, Fedelma Simms, took over the task of proofreading from my late husband, Donal, on whom I always relied. They are a family with a keen eye for precision in writing. Her husband, Nicholas helped get the MS ready for consideration. I am very grateful to them all. Needless to say, any outstanding misapprehensions and errors are my own.

The people of Owermoigne, to whom I dedicate this book, have been wonderful. In the text I have used surnames only for known public figures and elected officials or for people whose family heritage is important to the narrative. I use Christian names for all the others in an effort to protect their privacy. Dorset is a beautiful county and the village is surrounded by many areas of outstanding natural beauty and historic interest. It is perhaps what makes Dorset so special to the people who live there or the people who visit.

Rita Cruise O'Brien, 2014

Prologue – Four people

George, Lord of the Manor, Moignes Court, often brought a basket of apples to welcome neighbours when they arrived in the village. His wife and daughter remember him also unloading vegetables from the back of the car after Sunday service. There always seemed too many in the garden. One could see, from across a crowded room at the Court, that George had been a soldier by his demeanor, posture and height. He often said that he had a fine balanced life: twenty years in the artillery; twenty years farming; and twenty years in retirement. As the local lord, he was very involved in the village, the church and the parish council. People were very fond of him, and mourned his passing in 2008.

Margaret was born in Dairy Cottage in 1933. Her father did hedges and ditches around the village. When he died the family was very poor, but she described her childhood in the village as a very happy one, free to roam with a band of children. She remembers bitterly the cap doffing of her early years indicative of rural class and station, but for years has served on the parish council together with the current incumbent on the estate. As a local civil servant, she always championed the plight of the less fortunate in the county. Every year she joins the nearby march in memory of the Tolpuddle Martyrs.

Norrie lived in a house at the end of the village, established as a chicken farm after the war. She lived to the age of nearly 105 and merited a substantial obituary in *The Times*. As a young girl she had small parts in the Hardy Players, a local group of actors who performed dramatisations of Hardy's novels in the 1930s under the novelist's direction. She devoted her life to memories of Hardy and the Players, giving countless interviews for TV and radio. She attended all Hardy commemorative functions locally. Shortly after her hundredth birthday and in her honour, the New Hardy Players were formed, following years of her insistence. She played in their first performance of *Under the Greenwood Tree* in the village hall.

Pam, George's wife, was the daughter of a wealthy London stockbroker and through her mother was related to one of the first families of Dorset, the Popes, proprietors of the largest brewery in the county. In June 2009 Pam gave a five-minute summary of her early life to fifty members of the Monday Club in the village hall. It was the story of a privileged childhood in St John's Wood, with nannies, nurseries, cooks and in-house dumbwaiters for food delivery. Afterwards she wondered aloud to me if it had not been too privileged for the occasion. But then, she reflected, "We are now all the same."

Owermoigne and Surrounding Area

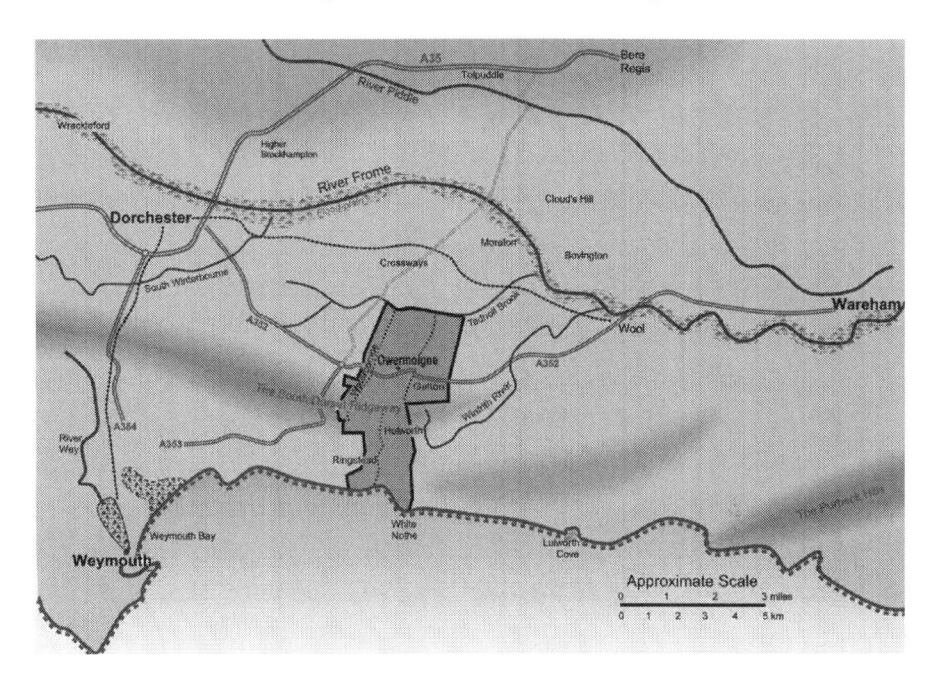

The Village Green

Introduction to Owermoigne

These are Owermoigne people. This book is about them and their lives in a village of about 470 people a few miles from the Dorset coast and seven miles east of the county town of Dorchester. The village is nearly 2,000 years old settled originally by Celts during the Iron Age, later by Romans who conquered the local tribes. The manor of the village was awarded to a Norman knight named Le Moigne sometime after 1066. Owermoigne is listed in the Domesday Book. The name of the village is unusual (Celtic and Norman) and is a story in itself, having become a source of controversy in recent years among linguists expert in the ancient place names of England.

Following its early foundation, Owermoigne was a feudal, then tied agricultural village until 1926 when the village houses and land were sold at auction. Dorset was for centuries known for the depths of rural poverty, where crops were worked with the simplest tools, much later than elsewhere in England or the rest of Europe.[1] The bleak situation gave rise to rural unrest in the 1830s and the formation of the first trade union to protest against working conditions in agriculture most notably at Tolpuddle, four miles from the village.

The village and farm buildings of Owermoigne were initially located behind the manor, Moignes Court, but were moved to

---

[1] Barbara Kerr, *Bound to the Soil: A Social History of Dorset*, 1750-1918, EP Publishing, Ltd. 1975, p. 25.

their present location in the early fourteenth century. Several decades before the plague came ashore at Weymouth, seven miles from the village, the wetlands behind the manor were deemed unhealthy. The foundation of St Michael's Church marks that event, as well as the appointment of the first Rector, William Chandos in 1333. In those days, the people of the village would have celebrated traditional feast days for ploughing and sheep shearing; the liturgical year followed Rogantide, Candlemas, Shrovetide, Lent, Easter, Maytime, Whitsuntide, midsummer, etc as well as a host of other festivals, mysteries, processions and saints' days. The upkeep of the church, the well, bridges and footpaths was organised collectively by the local squire and alms were raised to pay the Rector. There was a court at the manor, hence the name Moignes Court, where the lord sat in judgement over local disputes until 1902. The village was home to the people who worked on the estate, adding a blacksmith, carpenter, thatcher and finally a post office by the mid nineteenth century.

Owermoigne lost many of its young people to larger towns and cities soon after the railways arrived in Dorset in the 1880s. Thomas Hardy wrote a story about the village which he called Nether Moynton. "The Distracted Preacher" was based on the notorious centuries old practice of smuggling along the coast. His villagers hid the brandy casks in the old church tower but were eventually brought to book. Following World War I rural churches remained the centre of local activity until village halls were built – in Owermoigne in 1937. Dorset saw considerable action early in World War II as Weymouth and all the coastal areas were strafed by German bombers. An airfield a few miles from the village was often hit and in 1944 American and Canadian troops were billeted locally in preparation for the D-Day landings from Weymouth.

Class distinctions were very marked in England's rural villages which were well recalled in Ronald Blythe's classic account of an English village in Suffolk, *Akenfield*, published in 1969.[2] Dorset was no exception. Following the war, Margaret recalled that people may have been dissatisfied with their lot but they were reticent about complaining for fear of losing their jobs and the income which supported their families. She remembers her father still doffing his cap to Cecil Cree, the local squire. By the time of his son, George Cree, attitudes had begun to change. The family were decidedly more approachable largely because George had served abroad in the army for two decades and brought fresh ideas to the village. He was also a working farmer. Margaret served on the parish council with George's son, Martin, a local businessman, for years. They share a great mutual respect despite being keen supporters of opposing political parties.

The people of Owermoigne today have chosen to live there, that is most of them are incomers, arriving in successive waves since the early 1960s. In 1983, Betty, who headed a WI

---

[2] Published in 1969, London: Penguin Books. The village was somewhat smaller than Owermoigne (298 people in 1969, it had grown to 400 by 2006 when a sequel was written). Blythe wrote a portrait of a traditional village frozen in time. Thirty-five years later, Craig Taylor, *Return to Akenfield*, London; Granta Books, 2006 lamented the passing of the traditional village occupations and crafts. I have not used extensive verbatim interviews as they did and my story is not a lament for the old days, rather a tale of sociability and social mobility in a contemporary village in rural England.

Project on the history of the village, wrote a short poem for its publication:

> *Peopled now by strangers.*
> *Not Owermoigne born and bred*
> *Who run shoulders*
> *with the local folk*
> *And in harmony*
> *are wed.*
>
> *Most of us newcomers have*
> *come from far and wide. We*
> *took one look at Owermoigne.*
> *And thought we'd like to bide*
> *And roam no more, but in its beauty hide.*[3]

Local people did not realise how few people who live in the village were born there, or even in Dorset. They have never considered it: people just seem to have folded into village life from the 1960s onwards. I found only two people who were born in the village and still live there, but perhaps even more surprising only a few people who were born in the county. During the war, incomers were servicemen and Land Girls. There followed people who came to work at the nearby Atomic Energy Authority installation at Winfrith during the days of nuclear threat at the height of the Cold War. These engineers and technicians came from London, Manchester, Leeds and Sheffield and brought with them great enthusiasm for activities and social life in their new home. While many rural villages like Akenfield remained unchanged even in the 1960s, Owermoigne moved on, thanks to the influx of

---

[3] The Owermoigne Women's Institute, *Owermoigne: a History*, unpub. 1983, inside cover.

incomers like Jerry, William, Stuart and their wives who created the beginnings of a new social life which thrives until today.

These new arrivals were followed in later years by retired people like Dulcie who had been a headteacher and Alex, a garage owner. They were from equally distant locations and brought with them similar enthusiasm, energy and most significantly, precious time. National policies have in recent decades favoured the promotion of voluntarism and community activities in villages, towns and cities, whether called the Big Society or the Third Way. But the people of Owermoigne never required the assistance of official promotional schemes. They did need funds to refurbish the church and village hall which came from local and national assistance schemes. And thanks to people like Geoff, the church treasurer, and Bob, the chair of the village hall, they succeeded wonderfully in recent years raising money from a variety of sources.

This small village without a post office, shop or pub has created a surprising range of local social activities. Owermoigne is not a posh village, unlike some of those in the northern part of Dorset. There are only a handful of houses of substantial size although a high proportion of houses (83 per cent) are owner-occupied, higher than the local average.[4] A few are holiday accommodation or B&Bs. Only about fifteen households are without cars. I was initially drawn to write about the village having been impressed by its vitality and

---

[4] 2011 Census Parish Profile, Dorset Environment Directorate, Dorset County Council, September 2013, n.p.

range of social activities available to all. The origin of this book to explore why and how this social activity came to be and how ilt has been sustained for more than a half century. My exploration into the subject revealed a radically different portrait to the grinding poverty Dorset people had suffered for centuries. It is a story not only of sociability but of quite remarkable social mobility.

A Personal Note

My husband, Donal and I were part of the wave of incomers to Owermoigne. We found it to be a very welcoming place when we bought a house in the village. We moved into a rare second home in this village. But we found a lack of the resentment felt about second home owners whose presence adds pressure on property prices, often putting them above the level of local affordability.

Although somewhat remote strangers to the locality (as Irish, American, Londoners and weekenders) we quickly became very interested in the local people and their activities from the outset, stopping to talk to people along the footpaths and lanes of the village and attending local events. They were curious about us and we were equally so, about them. Donal sometimes remarked that Owermoigne people were so talkative and friendly that we might have been in rural Ireland.

Our choice of this village in Dorset had been in fact a compromise for not having a second home in Ireland where Donal was born and spent his childhood. While I was delighted at the prospect of "borrowed roots" as the wife of a returning son in an Irish village, Donal was never keen on the role, preferring the anonymity of being a migrant in London. He loved the English countryside, which we visited often before settling in Dorset.

We had good friends who had a cottage in a village north of Blandford Forum and were resolutely keen to introduce us to Dorset. They called it a "well-kept secret" as the county has no motorways and the train services were slow. House prices therefore had remained affordable. In the summer of 1998 the impetus for action arrived. After a disastrous holiday in Normandy with two elderly family members, we decided that it was about time to do something for ourselves. And so we did.

In July 2012, Donal died in the village after a long illness. Jill Lawton, the Church Warden, wrote in *Compass*, the parish magazine: "Many thanks to the Cruise O'Brien family, for having the good sense to have a house in Owermoigne and join the community. They loved the village and we in turn loved them as was shown by all those who attended the service to celebrate Donal's life in early August." No greater tribute of their friendship could be found.

Social Life in a Modern Village

Starting with the Labour administration in 2000, government has spent a great deal of money and policy time trying to create community cohesion schemes based on a somewhat fanciful re-imagined historic English village. At the heart of the Big Society and the Localism is something of a nostalgic longing for the rural arcadia of the village. Its romanticism has been rooted in the collective imagination since Victorian times when John Ruskin and Cecil Sharp among others ensured its importance and popularity. It has been revived in recent years with television series such as *Cranford* and *Lark Rise at to Candleford*.

Historic rural communities shared common labour, were related through extended family ties and shared the same saints' days. In the English village today, close family and friendship ties are found outside the village, often at some distance. The church has an important role, but it is no longer the pre-eminent focal point of life in the village as it had been until about 100 years ago. People are highly mobile with almost universal car ownership. They no longer gather around the village well. They have fridges and freezers which means that they do not depend on local supply – a good thing since the village lost its post office and shop in 2009.[5] The people of Owermoigne are not a community in a traditional sense; they have a great community spirit based on neighbourliness and shared social activities. But they live very separate lives and prefer it that way.

Owermoigne has had a series of social entrepreneurs like Betty who came to the village in 1977 from a boarding school in Dorset where she was the matron. A great admirer of Octavia Hill, she remains in her late eighties an avid social reformer. She and others were instrumental in bringing new ideas to the village and seeing them through, drawing kindred spirits around them. People seemed willing to volunteer their time and effort for different activities. Most

---

[5] Nearly 80 per cent of the villages in West Dorset have no post office since that date. Dorset County Council, "Rural Services Report," 2009.

club and activity decisions are taken democratically by majority vote. For a small village, Owermoigne has many prominent social clubs and associations. New ones like the Monday Club and the craft circle, the inspired idea of Pauline, an experienced craftswoman, are continually being created. The monthly parish magazine publicises future events and records past activities. Most clubs publish annual programme leaflets of their activities and there is a village website.

The strong sense of neighbourliness was never more evident than when the village shop closed. People worried that it would be difficult to keep touch with some of the older people, but this hub was quickly replaced by the newly invigorated practice of looking in on older people on a regular basis. Unorganised, it arose naturally among neighbours. Transport was and is arranged to village hall activities if people no longer drive. Shopping is done by neighbours if people are ill or very old. Some homemakers like Ann cook on a regular basis for elderly bachelors and widowers. Some of this activity is paid, some is voluntary, but most important it is available.

Nearly 30 per cent of the people in Owermoigne are retired and many are very old now, although 80 per cent of the people in the village report good health. This reflects the population profile of southwest England: Dorset has a higher concentration of older people than any other county.[6] And West Dorset is one of the ten local districts in the country

---

[6] 2011 Parish Profile, Op. Cit., Office of National Statistics, Eddie Smith, "Portrait of the South West", August, 2009, pp. 43, 47.

with the highest number of retired people.[7] It is perhaps no accident as 70 per cent of West Dorset has been designated "an area of outstanding natural beauty" with 79 conservation areas.[8]

A few years ago a national campaign and website was created called "Over the Hill".[9] It is intended to warn retired people that locating in an idyllic rural community can have serious downsides. Their factsheet points to "rural social deserts", a lack of local transport based on choice and control of life, shopping and health services. Highlighting some of the challenges of rural retirement, they identify isolation and loneliness as a potentially serious problem. While this is accurate in general terms, it does not greatly affect the older people in Owermoigne. Dorset launched a POPP (Partnership for Older People) programme, an inter-agency effort to try to improve the life and well-being of older people, following a Department of Health initiative in 2005. It aims to ensure that people are in good health, socially integrated and secure and safe. It tries to help with financial security and promote dignity. The local representative of the programme said that there was very little call for their services in the village.

The lack of medical, shopping or transport services had led some people to consider leaving the village, especially as there is excellent new accommodation in Dorchester, where one is in walking distance of most services. In a recent

---

[7] *The Times*, 13 September, 2013, p, 27 reporting on the 2011 census.
[8] Dorset County Council, Environment Directorate 2010, English Heritage, West Dorset District Council, 2009.
[9] The Rural Company Project, "Over the Hill: Wise Up to Rural Aging", Factsheet, accessed 15 March, 2013, www.overthehillcampaign.org.uk.

conversation on a footpath with Ida who no longer drives, she indicated that she intended to leave the village to re-locate somewhere where she could walk to a shop and enjoy some local entertainment. She relocated to Puddletown. Estate agents boasted to Val and her husband, when they were considering a move to the village from a lifetime of employment and residence on army bases, that the village had a very active social life. That interested them and Val became a very active secretary of the village hall and now serves as its chair.

The village has had its fair share of local disputes. In the 1960s, the village was split on the installation of street lighting. Newcomers were keen, but older residents did not agree and they won. The night sky remains quite spectacular from the village streets and torches are essential to get from place to place after dark. In 1987 a new house was planned in a prominent location in the main street but the owners, Wendy and Peter, changed their application to two houses on the same plot. About 70 people signed a petition against this change of plan, but the application went through and they were built. They found themselves cold shouldered until their drive was needed for the Street Fayre ice cream stall and Wendy was needed to prepare floral garlands for the church canopy. She and Peter do many things for the village and the rift quickly mended.

In 2007 a bitter dispute over the local playground arose and simmered for the best part of three years. It became very acid indeed as public meetings descended into shouts of abuse among neighbours who had known each other for years. The Parish Plan of 2005 had noted that there was little for children to do. The existing play area had become very dilapidated and older children seemed only to have the main street through the village to gather and ride bikes. A group was formed to raise funds for the playground among young parents, but the equipment proposed was regarded as garish and outsize, viewed from the village street below and from several houses. People passed one another in the lanes and turned the other way; friendships seem to have been shattered. It was mostly a generational dispute between young parents and older property owners whose homes looked onto the playground. But in due course it all simmered down and peace was restored, although one person recently commented that "it still left a little dirt on the wall."

There is always great concern that the social activities will not be maintained. The number of participants in the local Women's Institute, founded 68 years ago, is waning and a recent meeting to discuss forthcoming activities at the village hall only attracted two non-committee members. Current activists are always looking for younger people to take on the roles they have filled, but they seem much less interested. For the moment, things seem to be manned sufficiently to continue and a few younger couples have become involved. People do not seem to like coming to meetings or joining committees, but they are always available for events and entertainment in large numbers.

The sociability of Owermoigne is a rather conservative one, based on traditional social activities such as skittles and bingo, but no book club. And the village is overwhelmingly Conservative. There was some attempt to try to keep the village shop and post office open on a co-operative basis, as has been done in other villages with the help of the Plunkett

Foundation. But this suggestion by Charles, a successful entrepreneur, foundered largely through scepticism, as did a project to introduce a community wind power scheme. Some things just do not work. And sometimes big efforts like the street fayre fail to be maintained, possibly because limited numbers of people are willing to continue to do things or have the right sort of skills.

For thirty years the village had a biennial Street Fayre which raised great sums for local clubs and associations including the football team, the Owermoigne Owls. It was a significant summer event for the towns and villages around, with some local people in period costume. For years the Street Fayre was chaired by Graham, a retired business executive, but it was a big responsibility with almost a year of preparation. Graham could not get someone to take his place after serving in the role for ten years. The search for a new chair also occurred at the time of the playground dispute when the collaborative spirit of the village was at low ebb. That said, there were excellent celebrations for the Royal Wedding in 2011 and the Queen's Jubilee in 2012, a village tradition which goes back more than 100 years. Funds have been raised from the Heritage Lottery Fund to completely refurbish the pre-war village hall with a new roof, a fine new kitchen and spectacular handcrafted wooden doors. From the diocese and various church charities, the tower and roof of the church have been renewed.

What is social capital?

Some scholars writing about social activity claim that people live longer and are happier when they belong to groups and associations. Accordingly, belonging to a group can improve your health and your psychological equilibrium. There is some serious research on the matter, although the precise benefits of such fellowship are in fact almost impossible to measure.[10]

Prevalent concerns about the decline of community life were made popular by Harvard professor, Robert Putnam, in *Bowling Alone*, as he analysed the marked decline in American social activities.[11] Borrowing from economics (doubtless to add value or gravitas) this became known as the decline of social capital. Defined as the benefit derived from collective activity rather than a sum of individual activities, social capital as a concept appeared first in the work of Jane Jacobs on US cities in the 1960s.[12] Putnam, who sometimes referred to it as "sociological WD-40", initially worked on the differences in social and economic life between southern and northern Italy. He later applied his thinking to the decline of American clubs and other social activities and found that people in the US among other things no longer belonged to bowling leagues, but preferred to play alone, hence the title of the book. Owermoigne incidentally has an active skittles league and the annual championship played in the village hall is attended by more than 40 people.

Several surveys and research appeared to indicate that the British had developed a poor sense of trust and belonging. In 2008 the BBC and *The Daily Telegraph* reported a study

---

[10] Henry Hemming, *Together: How Small Groups Achieve Big Things*, London: John Murray, 2011, pp. 275-76.
[11] New York: Simon and Schuster, 2000.
[12] *The Death and Life of Great American Cities*, New York:Random House, 1961.

from Sheffield University which seemed to demonstrate that people were lonelier than they had been 30 years before. Writing about anomie[13] and suicide, they implied this rising trend was related to a lack of belonging or participation.[14] Membership in trade unions had declined as had traditional working men's clubs, Rotary and other lodges.

From the start of the new century, Parliament and Whitehall began to take an interest in the promotion of community. It was to become both prominent and fashionable in policy circles. A Defra publication, "Our Countryside: the future", declared that "community capacity was a goal in itself – that high levels of social capital in a community will result in higher levels of democratic engagement and civic action," and act as an antidote to problems of isolation and access to services.[15] The trend went hand-in-hand with buzzwords such as social capital, social cohesion and stakeholding. New Labour's agenda was underpinned by the need to try to build a strong attachment to place. It was largely a mistake to assume that this could be engineered from above. Community support officers were created and the Department for Communities and Local Government came into existence with a Cabinet position.

Following this trend, the search for social capital in rural Britain also became a theme of government sponsored research. A rural White Paper from Defra in 2002 created a research programme (the Rural Evidence Research Centre or

---

[13] Defined as alienation or purposelessness experienced by an individual.
[14] Hemming, Op. Cit, pp. 134-36.
[15] Department of the Environment, Food and Rural Affairs, Review of the Rural White Paper, 2004.

RERC) and an action group (the Commission for Rural Communities or CRC) to promote social capital in villages throughout England. The need to encourage a new rural quality of life became gospel in official circles. Was it an effort to stem the rural urban drift? If so, the evidence confounded their concerns.

From 2001-2011 the rural population of the South West and Dorset grew by nearly 7 per cent. The South West has the lowest population density and the highest proportion of older people in the country, with Dorset the highest of any other English county. The South West also enjoys the highest life expectancy for women (83 years) and the second highest for men (79 years).[16] This is attributed to healthier lifestyles.

It was not just older people who were on the move, altering the composition of rural villages. While young people between the ages of 16 to 24 were leaving rural counties to look for work, the 25–44 age group with young families became incomers in search of affordable housing. This was complemented by the opportunity to work at home promoted by distance working or the willingness to commute longer and longer distances to allow the family to live in a village environment.

Rural areas were not found to be a drag on the economy. The business start-up rate has been relatively high compared with urban areas, but some new enterprises tended to be

---

[16] Office of National Statistics, "Portrait of the South West", Op. Cit

short lived.[17] While employment in agriculture was in severe decline overall, there was a substantial increase in employment in services and knowledge-based industries, although wages were generally lower than in urban areas. There was a counter-urbanisation trend fuelled by the advance of technology and the internet in particular, and attendant changes in the composition of the workforce, flexible working practices and the rise in the employment of women. In recent years both the RERC and the CRC have been abandoned or transformed into environmental support groups.

In his book, Together: How Small Groups Achieve Big Things, Henry Hemming had initially sold his publisher the idea of the seemingly evident and popular theme of the decline of social activity, the demise of community in Britain. But, far from a decline in social capital, he found that community spirit in Britain was thriving. The pitch to his publishers on loneliness and the decline of group social activity morphed into a story about the value of togetherness. He found more than a million small democracies or associations and millions of events in community buildings each year. He found that there was no reduction in group memberships, but that associations had altered over the years. The old clubs gave way to 50,000 artistic associations, music societies, choirs, book groups, natural history societies and archaeological associations, many of which were enjoying exponential growth.[18] While some civic groups appeared to be

---

[17] Department of the Environment, Food and Rural Affairs, "Statistical Digest for Rural England," 2012, p. 112.

[18] Hemming, Op. Cit, p. 141.

on the wane, local sport was still as vigorous as ever.

Great attention to the official promotion of social capital in rural areas petered out, not only because of lack of interest, but because of cuts in public spending. Yet although a great deal of aggregate data was collected in this decade of experience there were few enough studies of particular villages to help give substance to the general claims. This book tries to address that gap.

Why and how does it work?

In Owermoigne social capital seemed never to be in short supply. Although there is no pub, there is a congenial drinking club. The Owermoigne Cricket Club (but no village pitch) was founded in the 1960s by the local team, the Mowers. With an annual subscription of £10 (recently raised from a £5 fee which lasted for many years), all villagers can belong. There are cosy premises next to the village hall with furniture made or donated by committee members. The bar is manned by the committee and drink is available at low prices.

A monthly Saturday market was started several years ago as a project to raise money for the village hall: it has contributed more than £10,000 to that cause in a decade of activity. Twelve stallholders sell anything from vegetables to handicrafts, antiques and bric-a-brac. The stall which sells out first is home baking. The market is very popular: most people stop for a cup of coffee and an opportunity to talk to neighbours. The Monday Club was created more recently to become an afternoon activity in the hall when nothing else was going on and to attract more men to its meetings. Recent activities in the hall or on local coach trips have been joined by as many as 30-40 people.

This is social capital. It is connections among people, linkages or networks which may be based on reciprocity. The linkages can generate trust which enables people to commit themselves to the group. Networks facilitate coordination, communication and help with the resolution of problems. They reduce opportunism. In some villages the parish council has a central role and acts as a catalyst of social activity, but in Owermoigne the central role is the village hall. In 2000, 85 per cent of villages in England had a hall or community facility. Some are active; others perhaps are not.

Factors which facilitate and nurture social capital are an open welcoming culture, good lines of communication, informal structures so people can meet easily and meeting places. When there is a fund of social capital people can be mobilised to do things quickly. Owermoigne has demonstrated that success breeds success. But it has not always been so. Troubles like the playground dispute placed the social capital fund temporarily in deficit and contributed to the cancellation of the Street Fayre.

Social capital works better when there is not a great disparity of income among people, which is true in Owermoigne. The movement of substantial numbers of middle class people into a village en masse can sometimes destroy the sense of community which they may seek and value. In the 1960s when Owermoigne had an influx of middle class incomers they initially created activities such as cricket, excursions and social clubs but welcomed others to join. Prior to their arrival there had been little activity and the opportunity was welcomed rather than overwhelming what had gone before. This was also true in Broadmayne (pop. 1,000) which is part of the local benefice. In contrast the village of Stourpaine in north Dorset (also pop. 1,000), which is divided between the manor houses and farmhouses in the old centre of the village housing the middle and upper middle class and the large social housing estate across the main road, has some difficulty generating local social activities.

Factors which limit or erode social capital occur when a small group of highly committed people "run the show" which often hinders others from wishing to take part. Although the founder social entrepreneurs in Owermoigne sometimes stay on longer at the head of activities than they ought, some accommodation is usually found by way of honorary titles or positions. Surprisingly there appear to be no factions or close knit cliques which have formed in the village. There are friendships but no cliques. An over-50s preserve of social activity can keep younger people from joining. The generational split of the playground dispute left many of the younger people involved in promoting its renovation unwilling to join other activities. In fact, though, the younger couples have jobs and are occupied with young children which tends to mean that they have less time to devote to village activities unlike retired folk. Only the Owermoigne Cricket Club and the Owls football team appear to be genuinely multi-generational activities in the village.

In some instances the closure of local schools (2006 in Owermoigne) and post offices (2009) have had a negative effect on village activities. The village children now go to a new school a few miles away in Crossways with a campus and playing fields. Crossways does not have a historic foundation. It was is not a traditional village, rather built and settled mostly after World War Two and allowed to spread into the available land which was once the wartime airfield at Warmwell. The old Victorian single room schoolhouse in Owermoigne had been bursting at the seams with prefab outbuildings and had no school grounds for play. People from the village meet at the post office in Crossways and enjoy convivial conversations. But both the shop and the post office are greatly missed.

In Owermoigne congeniality and a collaborative spirit have further muted class and status considerations. The women who work as daily cleaners in the village are committee members of the Women's Institute or serve on the parish council. A small independent builder became the moving spirit behind the new playground renovation.

Moving On

Owermoigne one hundred years ago was a tied agricultural village – all houses and land belonging to the manor. (See map of the period and today.) The lives of agricultural workers and their families in Dorset were particularly hard, well recorded by local historians and dramatised by Thomas Hardy. The poverty, disease and squalor of those years led to the first agricultural revolt and workers' union in Tolpuddle in 1832. Any historical source on the subject brings this deplorable period to mind. The village was sold in 1926. Dorset County Council was looking for the opportunity to provide much needed rural housing and overcome overcrowding. The council made the land available for purchase and development, while building some much needed public housing on the main road into the village. Yet, there were still some old thatched dwellings with earth floors until the 1960s.

There are a few defining periods in the history of Owermoigne. The first is the early settlement of Celts, Saxons and Romans. The second is the feudal era, the enlargement of the estate and the settlement of the village in its current location. The third would be the rebuilding of the church after the mid-nineteenth century and the foundation of the local school by the rector, John Robert Cree of the local landed family. The village and its farming occupations changed little until after World War I. Following the events of the Second World War, there was a great transformation in local life and the activities of incomers in the 1960s enlivened local activities. This is the fourth defining period, while the population has remained relatively stable since the mid-nineteenth century.

More than seventy people were interviewed in Owermoigne and the nearby hamlet of Holworth as well as neighbouring farms in Galton and Watercombe, which represents more than 15 per cent of the local people. Only a handful of people declined to be interviewed. The stories of these people are told in thematic categories reflecting the activities of the village. Theirs is a story of lively and abundant social activity. The chapters outline the circumstances and contributing factors which have made it possible. Does it represent a common thread throughout England? Or are villages like Owermoigne more prevalent in certain counties and regions?

The Village at the End of the Nineteenth Century

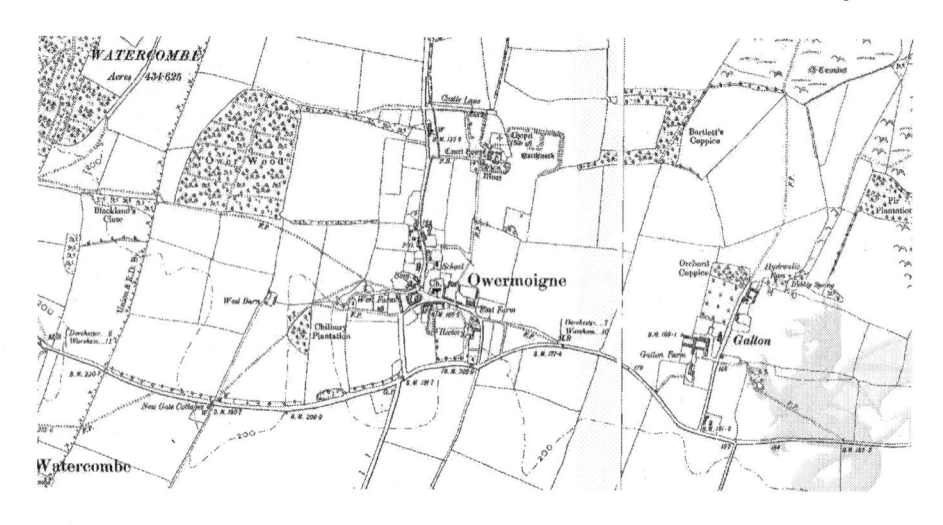

The Village Today

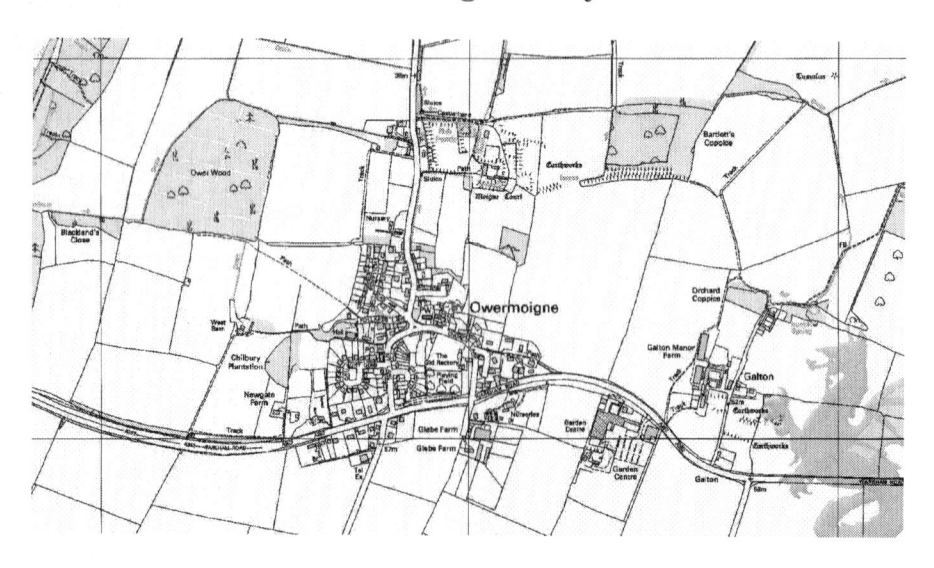

Chapter One

From the earliest times to the estate and village

What's in a name? Celts and Romans

From the earliest times, Owermoigne has been a village of incomers. The first homesteads were probably Celtic, later Roman, then Saxon. Once a system of farming was established under Saxon rule, the village grew very slowly through the medieval period and later tenancies on the estate. The name of the village is Celtic and Norman which has led to nearly a hundred years of speculation about its prefix "Ower". Moigne is more obvious, derived from the name le Moygne, a knight from Lower Normandy who was probably awarded the land shortly after the invasion in 1066. The records are found in the Domesday Book (1086) and in the reign of Henry I (1100-1135).

Why is the origin of the name of this small village so interesting to linguists and historians? It is an example of a rare survival of a Celtic or Brittonic place name from the Iron Age. Where there are little or no archaeological remains which can tell a story, linguists have begun to fill the void for this era. It was a time when the Romans conquered the local tribes and very few of their place names survived. "Ower" is a tenacious small fragment of history behind which there is an interesting story.

The earliest known excavations in Dorset reveal Stone and Bronze Age remains, including numerous barrows. These ancient people were later superseded or taken over by Iron Age tribal groups related to the inhabitants of Wales and Cornwall, with whom they shared a common Celtic language. The Durotriges built Iron Age forts and earthworks in which they lived, farmed and kept their livestock. They are also found in Wiltshire and Somerset, but their largest and most celebrated construction is Maiden Castle just outside modern Dorchester. The Durotriges were a loose confederation of smaller tribes which minted and used coins (silver with simple designs, but no inscriptions) prior to the Roman conquest.[1] The early Britons traded with Gaul, particularly selling their pottery from the excellent natural harbour at Poole (and so it continues today as the well-known Poole Pottery).

At the time of the Roman invasion, the Durotriges were said to have "put up a spirited fight" at Maiden Castle according to Sir Mortimer Wheeler, a renowned archaeologist working in the 1930s. But current opinion among scholars is that most of the local sites fell with ease to the invaders. The Durotriges were conquered by the Roman Second Legion under General Vespasian in AD 43, moving in from the coast at Poole and by land from Winchester. It is a noteworthy historical touch that Dorset County Council offices were until recently located in Vespasian House, and in the grounds there are the remains of a Roman house with mosaic floors. After the conquest the Romans created a *civitas* called Durnovaria and incorporated Durotriges people into their

---

[1] www.dorset.co.uk/history/prehistoric_dorset.html, accessed 24/09/2009

settlement.

Traditional accounts of the Roman invasion in southwest England focus on the subjugation and killing of the local people, but they are not the whole story. Very little of the traditional Brittonic (Celtic) language was subsequently used, as Latin became dominant among the subservient tribes, particularly among people of importance. Most of the other tribal people would probably have continued to speak their own language, but there is no evidence that their Celtic language was written. A few place names survived, but most were lost as villages were scattered and the dwellings ephemeral.[2] The gradual withdrawal of the native language suggests the hegemony of Latin. They were likely enslaved, rather than facing massacre or ethnic cleansing. Flight across the Channel did give rise to settlements in Brittany and the Breton language, closely related linguistically to the Celtic language used in Wales and southwest England.

The surviving Celts, albeit a conquered race, probably had a more developed culture than the later Saxon invaders, owing to 400 years of Romanisation and the use of Latin. In the 200 years following the withdrawal of the Roman legions, the land which later became Dorset was an independent Romano-British kingdom, which held off the Saxon advance for a long time. The ancient Britons remained ethnically and legally a distinctive people deep into the recorded Anglo-Saxon period, which may imply that they continued to be Brittonic speaking, although Old English has few

---

[2] Richard Coates, "Invisible Britons: the View from Linguistics," in N.J. Higham, ed.*Britons in Anglo-Saxon England*, Woodbridge: The Boydell Press, 2007 pp. 172-91.

contributions from Brittonic in grammar or sentence structure. They do remain a legally distinct people until about 928 when a rebellion in the West Country was suppressed by King Athelstan.

The name "Ogre" for the area around Owermoigne appeared in the oldest maps of the area and is so listed in the Domesday Book in 1086. The continuing arguments about its origin have given welcome attention for the village. Most controversially, a Swedish scholar suggested that ogre meant "terror ridge" in the local Celtic language from *orora* (*oga* – terror; *ofer* – ridge).[3] Why the ridge might have had this designation is not known. It might have been a place of execution or of war calamity. There is evidence of human sacrifice in the area, and the later name of Gallows Hill for the road leading to the hamlet of Holworth a mile south of the village might suggest the continued use of the location for terrible deeds (although many local Dorset lanes bear the same name).

An alternative translation, suggested by Richard Coates, a distinguished British linguist, is that ogre meant "wind gap". There is a chalk ridge between the village and the sea, which is likely to have been an ancient settlement and road. Holworth today sits on top of that ridge and the road up to it constitutes a small wind gap.[4] There are several other ancient wind gaps in the vicinity which form a break in the uplands, notably at Poxwell, a few miles to the west. It

---

[3] Gillis Kristensson, "The place-name Owermoigne", *Notes and Queries* (Oxford University Press) March, 2000, pp. 5-6.
[4] Richard Coates and Andrew Breeze eds., *Celtic Voices, English Places*, Stamford: ShaunTyas, 2000.

might have been easier and safer in those times to have made one's way along a bald chalk ridge, rather than in the forest below.

There is no evidence of a Celtic settlement in Holworth, but there are remains of a medieval village in a hollow below the chalk ridge along a stream which consists of pits and ditches where some pottery shards have been found. The land was held by Milton Abbey, ten miles from the village and became a respite home for monks from 933, but this and the small village were abandoned between the fifteenth and the seventeenth centuries. In its earliest form, it was Holeworthe (934) and became Holverde in the Domesday Book meaning "enclosure in a hollow".[5]

Archaeological research behind the manor house of Moignes Court (1971-73) revealed the foundations of a village, together with earthwork ditches, cattle enclosures and pot shards. Beside the foundations of the manor house, the remains of a Roman-British settlement were found two years later, including silver coins and glass bottles.

The Saxons and the Domesday Book

After the Roman occupation of Britain and the withdrawal of the legions, Christianity was retained among the local people, henceforth known as "Celtic Christianity". The Saxons advanced very slowly into southwest England. It was largely an internal expansion from the eastern parts of

---

[5] The original site of the village was nearer the coast where there is a hollow and today a fourteenth century thatched barn, preserved by the National Trust.

Britain, long settled by these Germanic people. They simply drifted west and established a pattern of farming and settlement. They were pagans and succeeded in largely eradicating early Christianity from the lands they occupied: their loyalty and beliefs were rooted in family and community. In 790 following raids throughout Europe, the Vikings landed for the first time in Britain on the Wessex shore with three longships. "A Saxon official from Dorchester rode to greet them and ask their business. They killed him on the spot."[6]

The Norsemen continually invaded southern England for over a century thereafter, having established themselves in the northern part of Britain. It had murderous consequences for the local farming communities. To take an example, in 2009, during the excavations for a new road between Weymouth and Dorchester (in connection with the 2012 Olympic sailing) an earth-moving machine exposed a mass grave of fifty young men who had been decapitated with swords and axes at a time when the area was often pillaged by Viking raiders. It has recently been established (by DNA samples) that the remains were indeed Norse invaders from the sea or settlements in the North of England.[7] The widespread anarchy thereafter led to the fortification of castles and monasteries.

Defences by the Saxon kings, particularly Alfred the Great of Wessex (878-889), consisted principally of earth ramparts

---

[6] Simon Jenkins, *A Short History of England*, London: Profile Books, 2011, p. 29.

[7] Work on the site is ongoing, Dorset County Archaeology Dept.

around settlements, like those in Wareham which are still visible to this day. In 876 Alfred led soldiers to relieve the monastery at Wareham: he was a fervent Christian, literate in Latin and ancient Saxon, who had made a pilgrimage to Rome in his youth. Once settlements were fortified, the Wessex kings built castles and monasteries. While the Vikings occupied East Anglia and the North, Wessex put up a serious defence under Alfred. He led his forces to victory over the Norsemen in 878. Harold, the last Saxon king, fought for his land against the Normans at the Battle of Hastings. Land ownership was later recorded meticulously in the Domesday Book, essential to William the Conqueror, following the Norman invasion. It was a record of land, livestock and other holdings, intended to raise tax revenue to build defences in order to protect the realm from further invasion. This was codified in 1086 under King William as a survey of the geography of the realm, to establish title and value for taxation and end disputes among his barons.

"Ogre" had been held by John, the Dane, the Domesday Book tells us. By 1086, the land may have been owned by the Le Moygne family but was in the charge of Matthew of Moretagne, who also held land at Meleburne (Milborne St Andrew). Le Moygne means monk in French and the family crest represented a demi-monk with a penitential whip in his hand. The family came from Mortain in Lower Normandy which may have provided a name for the neighbouring village of Moreton. Simon de Moygne is said to have defeated a poorly equipped Saxon army at Watercombe Farm on the edge of the village where the dead of both sides were buried in tumuli nearby. From the reign of Edward I (1272-1307), the family held the title of "Sergeantry of the Kitchen", providing services to the King for banqueting and food preparation.[8]

The Ogre estate, as recorded in the Domesday Book, consisted of 1,170 acres and seven plough teams (of eight oxen each). There were six serfs and seven freeman labourers, together with a watermill, meadow and pasture land worked by serfs and seven freemen. To support the men in armour, labourers owed most days of the year in work, after which they could tend to their own small plots and animals. They worked the fields from dawn to dusk; their wives did weaving and prepared food. People brought their corn to the lord's mill and could not leave the manor without his permission. The ancient watermill in the village operated until the end of the nineteenth century. At that time Dorset watermills, which numbered 280 in the early 1800s, finally fell into disuse, as it became more economical to centralise milling in larger installations. The mill house of the village and surrounding land became a farm, and after the Second World War a market garden and then a plant nursery.

The Origins of Moignes Court

In the reign of Henry I (1100-1135) the manor was held by Robert Moyne. William le Moigne was confirmed in feudal title to the land in recognition of his military services to King Henry III (1216-1272). He was given leave by Henry to build and fortify a house in 1267 "with a good dyke and stone wall,

---

[8] John Hutchings (Rector of Holy Trinity, Wareham), *The History and Antiquities of the County of Dorset*, 1774, 1831 (3rd edition), p. 454.

Owermoigne in the Domesday Book

The same [Mathew of Mortagne] also holds OGRE. John held it in the time of King Edward. It paid tax for 10 hides less 1 virgate. There is land for 8 ploughs. On the lords land are 2 plough-teams; 6 serfs; 7 villeins; 6 *coscets* with 5 plough-teams. There is a mill paying 6s. 20 acres of meadow. 1 league [12 furlongs] of pasture in length, half a league in width. The value was, and still is, £10.

The King holds WATRECOME. Aelfric held it in the time of King Edward. It paid tax for 1 hide. There is land for 1 plough. There is 1 *coscet*; half [share of] a mill paying 4s. [There is] pasture 1 league long, 1 furlong [wide]. It pays 15s.

The same B[rictwin] holds GAVELTONE. He himself held it in the time of King Edward. It paid tax for 2 hides [&] 1 and a half virgates. There is land for 2 ploughs. On the lords land is 1 plough-team; 3 serfs; 2 villeins; 6 *cotars*; There is a mill paying 12s 6p. 2 acres of meadow; 8 furlongs of pasture in length, 3 furlongs in width. The value is 40s.

Osmund the baker holds in GA[VE]LTONE. 1 hide [&] half a virgate. Four free men held it in the time of King Edward. There is land for 1 plough. There are 4 men paying 12s 4d. The value was 15s.

The church itself holds HOLVERDE. In the time of King Edward it paid tax for 5 hides. There is land for 5 ploughs. Of this the lords land is 3 hides where there are 2 plough-teams, 4 serfs; 4 villeins; 5 *coscets* with 2 plough-teams. There are 3 acres of meadow; pasture 5 furlongs in length, the same in width. The value is £3, [and] a sester of honey.

43

Owermoigne and local area from the Domesday Book

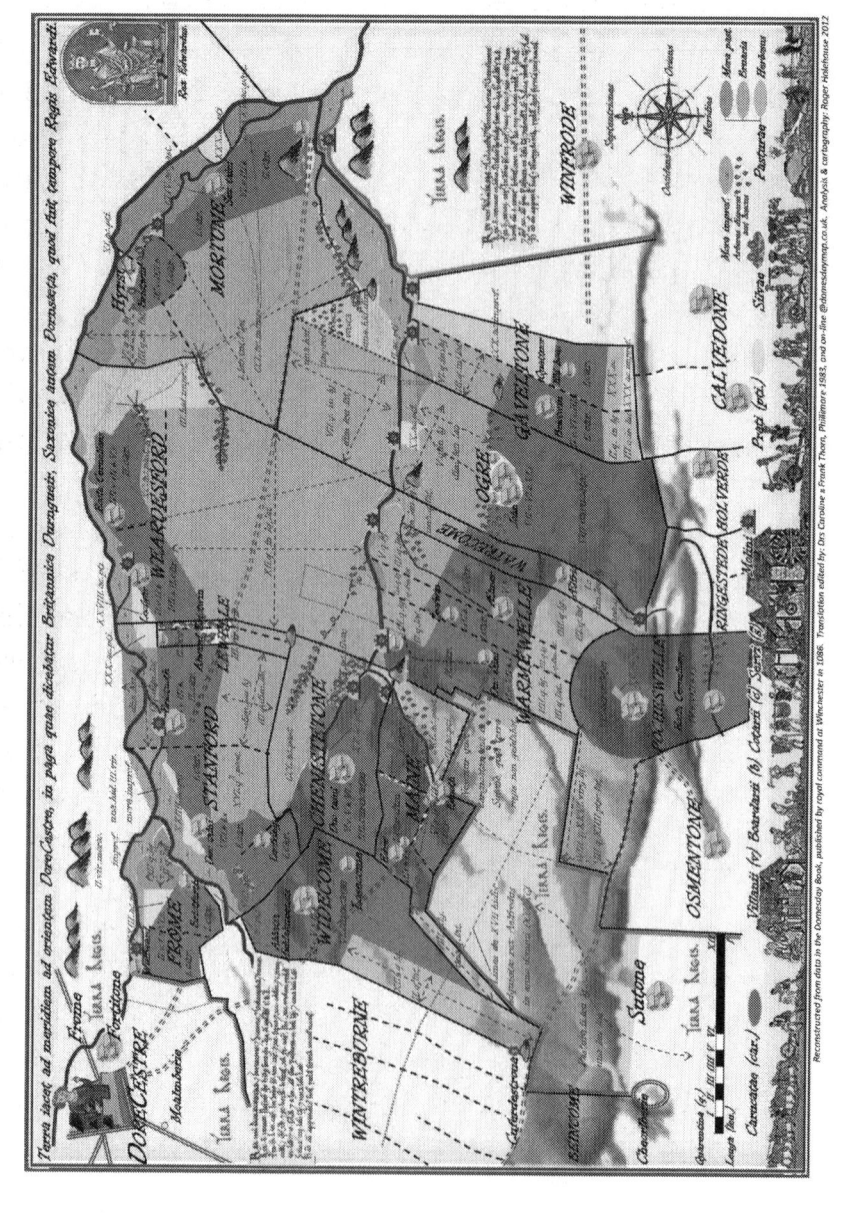

but without crenulations",[1] battlements on the parapet of the house, a feature reserved for those of higher status or title. At some point there was a chapel separate from the house. As the family and their successors had several estates, it was unlikely that the title holders lived at the manor for any length of time. For 700 years one absentee landlord after another took possession of the estate. It was their bailiffs and overseers who lived at the manor. It is said to be the oldest continually inhabited dwelling in Dorset.

In the reign of Edward I the village name became "Ower". In 1278 in an investigation before the judges in Sherborne, William le Moigne claimed "the rights to administer justice, keep the gallows at Ores (Owermoigne) and Winford (Winfrith), to impound anything washed up on shore and to administer fines for breach of the statutory price of bread and beer."[2] It thus became a manorial court at that time. A handsome courtroom was built in the thirteenth century in a wing of the current manor house of Moignes Court. In his *Buildings of Dorset*[3] the architectural historian, Nicholas Pevsner, singled out the thirteenth-century windows of the courtroom as "the only feature worthy of note in the village".

The Le Moignes also held land in Gloucestershire, Wiltshire, Hertfordshire and Essex. The suffix "moigne" was added to the name of the village during the reign of Edward II (1307-1324). By then there were several fortified castles such as Corfe. Dorset, throughout this period, was popular among the

---

[1] Hutchings Ibid.
[2] Hutchings Ibid.
[3] With John Newman, Yale University Press, 1972

nobility for its hunting estates. The estate was held by the Le Moigne family until the end of the fourteenth century. There were terrible storms and a "mini ice age" in England which started in the spring of 1315 when torrential rains destroyed crops and caused widespread starvation. The land behind the manor, the dwellings of serfs and free labourers, became very wet and bog-like (drained finally by George Cree in 1971). A moat was added which was partly for drainage and partly defensive. It allowed for the construction of a new manor house at a dryer location.

The people who worked the land moved to higher ground, the present site of the village, about a quarter of a mile away. St Michael's Church was consecrated in 1333, under the patronage of John Le Moigne who appointed the first rector/clerk, Walter Chandos. Life in the village revolved around an annual procession of saints' days. Each of the local residents was required to contribute a tithe to the church. The tower of the original church remains, but the rest of the church became unsound and was rebuilt in 1883 with funds left in the will of John Robert Cree, the rector, and an ancestor of the present owner. The people of Owermoigne probably did not escape the Black Death in 1348. The rats which carried the plague to England came ashore at Weymouth, some seven miles away, where the population of the town was decimated. There is no record of what happened in the newly located village.

The next title holders of the land and manor were the Stourton family who took over when Elizabeth Le Moigne married Sir William Stourton in 1398. The family held land in Wiltshire and their son, John became an MP in 1421 and a baron in 1448. By that time feudalism was loosening its grip on the land. The Tudor king, Henry VII (1495-1509) brought about a significant break with his Anglo-Norman predecessors. In so doing a local man, John Morton served the king well by establishing the first effective administration of the realm. Morton, who came from the village bearing his name since Norman times gained a Regis suffix for the small town of Bere, a few miles away. He was Archbishop of Canterbury and Chancellor, the two most significant posts in Tudor England. He is principally remembered for two things. The first, "Morton's fork" is a maxim on taxation which held that if a noble lived frugally he could afford to pay his full taxes, and if lavishly, his apparent wealth demonstrated that he could as well. The second was the arrangement of the dynastic marriage between the Houses of Lancaster and York when Henry married Elizabeth of York, thus ending finally the War of the Roses. This event is commemorated on perhaps the finest parish church roof in England to be found in Bere Regis. Commissioned by John Morton, it commemorates the dynastic marriage with respective emblems as well as one for Morton himself and his image on the fine bosses of the carved timbers.

Just as the local area began to recover from the plague and the expenditure of the Hundred Years War, including skirmishes along the coast, the Reformation further threatened stability and economic growth. The local monasteries had been dissolved by Henry VIII and some of the towns were punished as heretical under Mary Tudor. At this time Moignes Court consisted of a walled courtyard, probably including a bakery, brewery and a dairy farm, attached to the main building. It also had a moat (a dry feature today). The walls of manor houses in this period were hung with cloth and tapestries representing hunting scenes, religious or allegorical subjects. Framed pictures had no place yet in the English manor, yet the walls were often painted.

In 1557 Charles, Lord Stourton, a staunch Catholic, who lived in Wiltshire and also held estates in Gloucestershire and Essex, was the perpetrator of a notorious dual murder. Sir Charles killed two neighbours from the Hartgill family, with whom he had a dispute. It was said for a long time quite mistakenly that he had buried them under the floor at Moignes Court. He was indeed guilty of the vile deed but the bodies were disposed of in Wiltshire. For a long time, writers about the manor have repeated this error, tainting Moignes Court with the evil doings, but perhaps it is time to put that tale to rest. Although he appealed to Mary Tudor, the Catholic queen, for pardon, Lord Stourton was hanged in Salisbury by a silk cord "in respect of his quality". His estate reverted to the Crown, but during the reign of Elizabeth I, the estate became the property of his son by an Act of Parliament.

Poverty and Charity

Before the sixteenth and seventeenth centuries there are few records of the ordinary people in the village. It could be described thus: "life for the majority was one of hard unremitting toil, a constant struggle to grow enough food to sustain themselves and their families during the long winter months. It was a time when the fertility of crops was low and when crops and animals as well as humans were ravaged by disease and completely at the mercy of the weather."[4] The poor soil of the chalk lands of Dorset were used for grazing. Very good quality wool was produced, enhancing the local earnings for some. Travellers in Tudor England remarked on the size of the flocks, unparalleled elsewhere in Europe.

There were a series of bad harvests from 1594 to 1597 which caused famine in the growing cities. But by then a Poor Law began to take shape in a long series of experiments and enactments. Relief was henceforth provided to struggling families as imported grain was distributed. While still meagre, these measures were an improvement on former times and better than anything for generations to come on the continent.[5]

From the seventeenth century "one aspect of life in which Dorset has been particularly fortunate is in the remarkable number of charities, endowments, alms houses, hospitals and foundations, which over centuries have done well to mitigate some of the worst poverty."[6] In 1653, Adam Jones of Holworth left his modest estate "for the use of the poor of the parish forever, to be distributed by the minister and church wardens".[7] His cottage and about 30 acres of land formed the basis of the Adam Jones Trust, the details of which are found on an old wooden plaque in the church. Three houses were built from the legacy in 1882 and were called Charity Cottages. They were sold in the early 1960s and the proceeds

---

[4] J.H. Bettey, *DORSET*, City and County Historical Series, 1974, p. 123.
[5] G.M. Trevelyan, *English Social History*, London: Longman.
[6] Bettey, Op. Cit., p. 132.
[7] Plaque in St Michaels's Church, Owermoigne.

reverted to the trust. A sum still remains in the trust for distribution to needy people in the village and is today valued at about £6,500. The trustees have traditionally been the rectors and the church wardens who handle the distribution with great discretion. With the improvement of living standards, the trust in recent years has developed from its origins of poverty relief. In 2011 grants of £100 were offered to college students in vocational or university courses for books or software.

The Civil War

Dorset was torn apart in the seventeenth century by civil war, with both nobility and commoners joining the fray. Towns like Weymouth were under the parliamentarians, while Corfe Castle, a royalist stronghold, fell to Cromwell's forces and was destroyed. Today its striking hilltop ruins have become a picturesque icon of Dorset. Tired of the destruction perpetrated by both sides, a group called the Dorset Clubmen was formed. In an ill-fated effort to protect crops and animals, they fought against both protagonists armed with clubs, pitchforks and scythes. 1645 was their last great battle with Cromwell's army. While thousands of local clubmen outnumbered Cromwell's troops by about four to one, they were defeated and fled, dismissed by Cromwell who referred to them as "poor silly creatures".[8]

Following the civil war, some local people were involved in the Monmouth Rebellion in 1685. In an attempt to overthrow

---

[8] Clubman Uprisings, 1644-46"
http://www.british_civil_wars.co.uk/glossery/clubmen.htm, accessed 24/09/2009; http://www.dorsets.co.uk/history.html, accessed 24/09/2009.

King James II, the pretender, the Duke of Monmouth (the eldest illegitimate son of Charles II) landed forces at Lyme Regis. The rebels finally met the Kingsmen in Somerset and were roundly defeated in the last battle in England to be fought with pitchforks. James sent the cruel Chief Justice, George Jeffreys to punish the rebels in what became known as the Bloody Assizes in Dorchester. Today the location of the trial is a tearoom, "The Judge Jeffreys," an odd remembrance of the wretched condemnation of 200 and the dispatch of another 800 to the West Indies.

Life in the Village and on the Estate in the Eighteenth Century

The homes of villagers in the eighteenth century generally consisted of one room, with walls of turf or unmortared stone stuffed with grass or straw. Chimneys and windows were rare, and the floor was bare ground. Cattle lived at one end of the room and people at the other with scant partition. The family sat on stones or heaps of turf round the fire with the smoke escaping through a hole in the thatch overhead. Men and women wore cloth which was usually spun and dyed at home. Children and many adults went barefoot. Men and women worked ill-drained soil, only half reclaimed from marsh. They returned to a damp home in wet clothes which they seldom changed. Rheumatism plagued and shortened their lives.

In 1703, the Stourton family sold Moignes Court to William Wake, a local man, who later became Archbishop of Canterbury. Shortly thereafter, in 1732, the ownership of the estate passed to Sir Theodore Janssen, of Dutch extraction, born in France, who arrived in London in 1680 with a legacy of £20,000 and made a further fortune in the City. His portrait by Hogarth together with his sons can be found in the Guildhall in London. He was a founder member/director of the Bank of England, and one of the wealthiest individuals in the country. He became a baronet under William III in 1715. By 1721, he had a fortune of nearly £250,000 and was the MP for Yarmouth.

Janssen became a non-executive director of the ill-fated South Sea Company, which benefited from his reputation as an excellent financier. The company which had been awarded a monopoly of trade between England and South America and was incorporated in the National Debt on the promise of 5 per cent interest payments. Shares in the company rose to ten times their original value and unleashed wild speculative, sometimes dodgy schemes. More and more shares were issued and huge paper fortunes were made. The directors were corrupt and inexperienced and the bubble burst, helped in part by the ongoing war with Spain, which jeopardised the British trading position in South America. The stocks crashed and people all over the country lost heavily. This included a substantial number of MPs and peers, but also porters and lady's maids who had bought their own carriages and found themselves suddenly destitute.

As limited liability companies had yet to be established, Janssen along with other directors became personally liable for the losses. Almost all the directors were arrested and their estates forfeited. Janssen as a non-executive director, however, was treated rather leniently compared to the others who faced complete ruin. He was allowed to retain £50,000 of his fortune, but was expelled from the House of Commons.[9] Stephen Theodore Janssen, his son, became Lord Mayor of London and an MP. He published a pamphlet, "Smuggling Laid Open". It was several decades before the British government under Pitt began to legislate and enforce anti-smuggling measures, owing to the massive losses to the Crown in excise duty from the West Country. But until the late nineteenth century, smuggling brandy and other spirits from France through the quiet coves of Dorset remained a major source of income to the people of Owermoigne.

Moignes Court had been left to the brother of the original Janssen millionaire. His daughter married into the Damer family and in 1826, the manor and 2,000 acres were sold by them to John Cree, Esq. His family were originally from Ennis in County Clare, Ireland. His uncle had made a substantial fortune as a free trader in East Bengal and purchased Thornhill House, near Stalbridge in Dorset. His nephew, John inherited the estate. When he sold it, he bought Moignes Court. At the time, the village already had 77 houses all of which belonged to the estate. They were clustered around the church, including East and West Farm Houses (18c) together with Dairy Cottage, the Old Forge and St Michaels, of older foundation.

Hardship and Rebellion

"The year 1750 is often taken as the high water mark of village prosperity in England. It was widely believed that

---

[9] John Carswell, *The South Sea Bubble*, London: Cresset Press, 1960.

after that date the peasant gradually lost his land, his grazing rights, his independence and his self-respect... (but) the foundations of the village seemed firmly set...."[10] This refers to the Enclosure Acts which came almost 100 years later to the village. Conditions for a majority of Dorset people worsened very considerably throughout the eighteenth century. For about 200 years the county was a byword for rural poverty. Bread and cheese was the staple diet of the labourer, washed down with tea or beer. They seldom saw meat but grew potatoes in their cottage gardens. There was a constant danger of sheer starvation owing to low earnings and high food prices. With the end of the Napoleonic Wars in 1815 and the recession in agriculture, conditions worsened still more. In that year, 13 per cent of the population of the county received poor relief, and the number forced to apply for help from each parish grew steadily.[11]

Rural England at this time was governed by the patriarchal rule of Justices of the Peace. They were appointed by the Crown and had functions which covered all aspects of country life, customarily supporting the rights of landowners. Removal orders could be brought against families if they required poor relief; they could be moved on if they had no right to settle in a parish. Several removal orders are on record for Owermoigne. Families receiving an order were escorted by a local constable to the parish boundary. They were ordered to return to their original parish, if they had one. There were also several "bastardy orders", issued by

---

[10] Barbara Kerr, *Bound to the Soil: A Social History of Dorset*, EP Publishing, ltd. 1975, p. 93, 95.

[11] J.H. Bettey Op. Cit, 1974, p. 136.

local JPs to compel a reputed father to pay maintenance and support for an illegitimate child (usually not named). Refusal to pay could result in a jail sentence.[12]

Dorset in the nineteenth century was an agricultural county where the people were slow to adopt new farming tools and techniques.[13] The Enclosure Acts consolidated large landholdings at the expense of smallholders. The enclosure came late to Owermoigne, not until the 1840s. The strip cultivation on many small parcels of land until then did not make it feasible to use early forms of mechanisation.

Local enterprise was beginning to develop, and some women were employed in button-making. Made initially from sheep horn and covered in fabric, they were later made from metal rings manufactured in Birmingham. Women and their daughters working at home often became the principal breadwinners of the family with greater earning power than their farm labourer husbands. The central depot for the button trade was Milbourne St Andrew, a few miles away which would have been thronged on Fridays with women bringing in their work and collecting payment. There were a few local schools at the time which specialised in teaching button-making.[14]

During the Napoleonic Wars (1795-1815) livestock were

---

[12] Various references, Dorset Archives, The History Centre, Dorchester, Quarter Session Books.

[13] Planting beans by hand and covering the soil with bramble sticks for support was common in Dorset, while it had already gone out on farms in Eastern Europe at the time, Bettey. Op. Cit p. 25.

[14] http://www.dorsets.co.uk/history/modern_social.html, accessed 24/09/2009.

moved ten miles inland from coastal pastures, as a means of preparation against a possible invasion. It did not materialise, but the erection of a series of beacons (prepared for lighting at short notice) along the South Coast served as an early warning system. These events in Dorset are chronicled in Hardy's *The Trumpet Major*, published in 1880. There was a severe agricultural recession following the Napoleonic Wars in 1815. Demobilised soldiers remained without jobs, which started a wave of protests. For the next fifteen years, widespread rioting was recorded in Dorset, including rick burning and the destruction of threshing machines. The movement spread throughout the local area. Great numbers of special constables were sworn in, and the yeomanry and coastguard were brought in to help quell the demonstrations. Vigorous precautions were taken by landowners to defend their property. By December 1830, troops arrived and the riots died down temporarily. A few improvements in wages secured in that year were quickly lost, and the local people were soon in as desperate a condition as before.

Following the Enclosure Acts farmworkers no longer had plots on which to grow vegetables nor open grazing land for their few cows and sheep. The enclosures enabled landowners to takeover vast acreages which had previously been available to local farmers and labourers. By 1830, appalling low wages, bad conditions and long hours of work stirred the Dorset farm labourers to protest. "The local wages of 9 to 10 shillings a week reduced families to starvation, partly exacerbated by very poor harvests in 1829 and 30. It was a time of unparalleled poverty, degradation and misery locally. This helped to fuel the explosion of outrage: many joined the widespread rioting and machine breaking that swept through southern England...."[15] In November 1830 farmworkers in Bere Regis assembled to demand better wages, and the movement spread to Wareham. Landlords were threatened. The country magistrates swore in great numbers of special constables to help quell the troubles and defend property. Men began to be arrested for unlawful assembly.

In 1833 George Loveless and his neighbours in Tolpuddle started a friendly society vowing not to accept work for less than ten shillings a week. They took an oath to join together to try to improve wages. They were arrested for swearing an unlawful oath. They were tried in Dorchester the following year and six found guilty and deported to Australia for seven years. Loveless had pleaded that they had broken no law, "...we were trying to preserve our wives and children from utter degradation and starvation."[16] Known as the Tolpuddle Martyrs, they garnered great support throughout the country and are credited with the formation of the first trade union in Britain. This is celebrated annually to this day with a local march and event, sponsored by the TUC. A row of charity cottages for poor farming families was built one hundred years later in commemoration of the events of 1833, and a local museum with a detailed history of the period was established. By this time, local people were seeking to put an end to the perpetual poverty of subsistence farming on very small plots.

---

[15] Bettey, Op. Cit, p.136.
[16] The Tolpuddle Martyrs Museum, 31 July, 2013.

Those who lost land because of the enclosures were compensated, although often with other land on poorer soil. In Owermoigne the new owners of the estate, the Cree family, obviously gained from the consolidation as their land increase in value. While the enclosures may have made agriculture more efficient, the social price paid for this consolidation was the rise in the number of landless labourers and a reduction of the amount of land for subsistence cultivation. There were very few independent landholdings as most of the area remained in estate ownership. Hardship and poverty persisted.

Chapter Two

Victorian Charity to World War Two

Farming and Trades in the Village

Evidence from parliamentary reports and royal commissions on Dorset continued to bear witness to the miserable working conditions of agricultural labourers and overcrowded cottages many of which were often deemed unfit for human habitation. It was not uncommon for local families to be living in buildings designed for animals. They grew their own food on small plots but were reliant on local mills for the cost of grinding their grain. There were few sanitary facilities and no public baths. Children were needed for work on the land; there were few village schools. The lot of farm labourers contrasted with great wealth on the estates, particularly by mid-century, a period of great prosperity for local landowners.

From 215 in 1801, the population of Owermoigne had doubled by 1850. Villages were isolated which gave rise to the growth of local crafts and trades. By 1841, the village had a shopkeeper, grocery dealer, carpenter, blacksmith and two shoemakers.[1] Until this time, labouring families baked their own bread and made their clothing and shoes. Carpentry served as a stand-by trade for local farm labourers. They

---

[1] Owermoigne Trade and Postal Directories, 1841-1915, Transcripts from the Dorset Reference Library, 2004
http://www.opcdorset.com/OwermoigneDirectory.htm

were often in demand for repairs to the church and the estate. The forge, now called the Old Forge, at the centre of the village would have supplied and maintained the equipment for the estate, including pumps and wagon fittings. The blacksmith would also have established a growing trade in latches, handles, pots and pans and hearth equipment for the local people.

Some of the occupations were shared with agricultural work. Every October from 1848, a village fair was held for the sale of cattle and horses. By 1855, there was a dairyman working on the estate, five servants at the house and three recorded at the rectory for the first time. At about this time, there were door-to-door deliveries by horse-cart including bread, cakes, fruit, vegetables, meat and fish. Somewhat later, hardware, coal and paraffin, drapery and services like shoe repair and knife sharpening were added, on horse-drawn carts from Dorchester and other nearby towns. By 1875 there were two thatchers. The post office was run by the Westmacott family whose daughter became the schoolmistress.

A local brickworks was built by the Cree family, as suitable brick clay was found above the local chalk beds. The brickworks supplied local building materials until the end of the nineteenth century, when cheaper bricks were brought by rail from Bedfordshire. There were also two chalk pits and a lime kiln in the village. The kiln made the quicklime used principally for fertiliser but also as building material for foundations and walls.

Owermoigne had (and has to this day) a stream running though it which had made the site attractive for the early settlement. Keeping the stream clean for local consumption was sometimes a problem. A court case in 1864 recorded that "no ducks or geese be allowed to run into the stream running though the village and that the Hayward [keeper of the village pound for stray animals] after giving notice do impound any so found and charge 2d for each duck and goose for his trouble."[2]

There were outlets from the stream for the supply of water. In the middle of the village was a "pile", recorded in old maps. It was a hard platform of bricks and rubble used for drawing water from the well beneath with a dipper. The pile became a meeting place and the location for planning of village events. It was located in front of the forge. There was a pipe supply for Moignes Court which ran along the bed of the stream.

Wetland agriculture along the many local steams was typical of the area. Wool, four miles away, is on the river Frome. Wetland agriculture was established there by the monks of Bindon Abbey at the end of the twelth century. Traditionally the meadows were flooded regularly in winter by "drowners" who ensured that the water was distributed through a series of wooden hatches. Starting in December, the flooding protected the grass from frost as it was needed for the lambs and ewes in early March. Then the cows grazed until the end of the year and the cycle began again. The flooding system began to die out around 1870 when chemical fertilisers began to be used to bring the grass on early in the season on the

---

[2] The Owermoigne Women's Institute, *Owermoigne: a History*, unpub. 1983, n.p.

chalk uplands.³ The local watercress industry was founded in 1892 in the wetlands north of the village. Originally packed in returnable flat wooden baskets, the crop today is packed in airtight plastic salad bags for sale in supermarkets. "Pulling" or cutting the crop which used to be done by hand is now fully mechanised.

The hamlets of Galton and Watercombe, both of ancient origin, were added to the parish as the land had been incorporated into the estate in the eighteenth century. Galton gave its name to a family of successful Quaker businessmen and intellectuals who became well-known in the industrial towns of the North.⁴ Watercombe was owned by the daughter of William Janssen in the eighteenth century. She was married to a son of the Earl of Dorchester. By 1875 Owermoigne had a parish clerk, who recorded meetings of the parish council and dealt with correspondence. Elected parish councils came twenty years later. Until this time travel between villages was very difficult, as the lanes would have been awash with mud most of the year.

By the 1870s agriculture was again entering a long period of depression. The drift away from the village was easier from the arrival of the railways in the 1860s and people were encouraged to leave Owermoigne to seek employment in the growing towns and cities outside Dorset. In 1889 the village population was recorded at 423. By 1895, it had dropped by

---

³ Alan Brown, *The Changing Face of Wool*, Wool: AG Brown, 1999, p. 94.

⁴ The most celebrated member of the family was the polymath, Francis Galton (1882- 1911), known principally as a eugenicist who also invented, among other things statistical methods, fingerprinting and an early weather map.

Village Children, late Nineteenth Century by the Forge and the Pile

Village Children

nearly 100 to 332.[1]

Smuggling as a Way of Life

Village incomes were supplemented by a thriving trade in smuggling brandy and other spirits. Thomas Hardy immortalised the smuggling activities of the village, which he called Nether Moynton in "The Distracted Preacher," to be found in his collection of short stories, *Wessex Tales* published in 1888. Hardy customarily spent time in the archives of the Dorset County Museum to research his stories. His reading of newspapers and other material found evidence of the plight of poor people and their exploitation, which he used extensively in his writings. Accounts of local smuggling were abundant. Hardy described the people of Nether Moynton as practising overlapping religious creeds, referred to as "trimmers", who attended chapel as well as the Church of England. In the story there are a set of comic turns when the newly arrived preacher tries to woo Lizzie, a local girl. They become caught up in the village enterprise of smuggling brandy from Cherbourg through Lulwind (Lulworth) Cove.

"There are tubs of spirit which have accidentally floated over in the dark from France," says Lizzie. "The kegs were as well known to the locals as turnips," Hardy commented. The story recounted merry scenes and deceptions and how the booty was stored in the church tower. The smugglers were described as labouring men – brickmakers, shoemakers and

---

[1] Bettey, *Op. Cit*, p. 140, Owermoigne Trade and Postal Directories, Op. Cit.

thatchers. The distracted preacher was predictably disturbed by the goings on and attempted to pry his love away from the illegal activities. He became "distracted" in the task, and did not succeed. The excise people came "sniffing" around the village hoping to earn a good price for apprehended local smugglers. Making a run for it, several villagers eventually emigrated to Canada. The preacher was called elsewhere to serve his ministry and returned to the village some years later to find Lizzie sunk once more into poverty. As in real life, the rectors of Owermoigne did not seem to have made much impact on smuggling. Perhaps they enjoyed the brandy.

In 1983 the Women's Institute in Owermoigne published a wonderfully researched history of the village for a national competition. They interviewed local people including an elderly resident who recounted this story her grandfather used to tell about smuggling in the village:

> *When he was young, he took part*
> *in the smuggling which was rife*
> *in Owermoigne. He and fellow*
> *smugglers*
> *were on their way back from Osmington with*
> *brandy barrels strapped to their backs, when*
> *they were shot at by the*
> *excise men, who had been*
> *lying in wait for them at*
> *Warmwell Cross. They got*
> *one better than the law*
> *enforcers and in fact tied*
> *them to trees before running*
> *off. No words were spoken*
> *or faces seen as the night*

was very dark so they were in no fear of identification. However when they reached the journey's end, great was their disappointment as all the brandy was gone; the shots had holed the barrels.[2]

The Estate and the Rector Benefactor

Moignes Court was purchased in 1827 by John Cree, Esq thus beginning the tenure of the family on the estate of nearly 200 years. The family are descendants of the McMahon, O'Neill and Creagh families of Ennis, Co Clare in Ireland. John Cree's uncle, who had no direct heir, had made the family fortune as a free trader in Dacca, East Bengal, India. He arrived there about 1765 on an East India Company vessel and quickly decided to leave the company employ. He had been John McMahon, but decided to use his mother's name, Creagh and simplified it to Cree (perhaps to be more easily understood by the native traders with whom he worked). Henceforth, this unusual spelling was exclusive to his descendants in England and America.

John Cree, merchant of Dacca, had an interesting career of nearly twenty years in India, dominated by trying to make a living independent of the East India Company. Together with other free traders, he railed against the Regulating Act of 1773 which tried to reinforce the company's monopoly. Having failed, he traded under the Danish flag and married the daughter of a company official.

---

[2] Owermoigne Women's Institute, <u>Owermoigne: A History</u>, 1983, n.p.

Once successful financially, he left for England in 1774 with his wife and family (two children born out of wedlock of a previous relationship in Dacca). Like many who had made their fortunes trading in India, John Cree sought to set himself up as a gentleman back home. He bought Thornhill House, an estate in Dorset and went to Dublin to establish a coat of arms for the family. He continued his involvement in trade with India under Danish protection, an illicit undertaking breaking the East India Company monopoly. He was described as a "self-important, pugnacious and confrontational character" from his earliest days.[3]

His son, James, who was also involved in the India trade, left his wife and sailed for America in 1798. This established the Cree line of the family in the United States, who continue to be very keen on the historic genealogy.

John McMahon was the nephew of John Cree of Dacca. He inherited the estate on the proviso that he changed his name to Cree. He sold Thornhill House and purchased Moignes Court in 1827. He was 48 years old at the time but lived to a great age with his family at the court. His eldest son was John Robert Cree, who became a great benefactor to the village in the late nineteenth century. He was born in 1806 and was a Trinity, Cambridge graduate. He became a "squarson", serving both as Rector of Owermoigne and the estate owner. His brother James was the rector in Chaldon, a few miles away but lived in the rectory in Owermoigne.

---

[3] "Biography of John Cree, merchant of Dacca" by Mike Spathaky, www.cree.name/geneologies/bio3269, 2010. The author's mother was member of the Cree family.

John Cree

Cree Coat of Arms

John Robert Cree

Moignes Court in 1876 showing the thirteenth-century

Originally built during the reign of Elizabeth I, the rectory is one the finest dwellings in the village. (See photo) It is a handsome walled property set back from Church Lane with a dining room built with timbers said to have come from a Spanish galleon from the Armada, wrecked in nearby Osmington in 1588.

John Robert Cree was a bachelor and made his home at Moignes Court. He donated the funds for a school for 80 children in 1873, which functioned for more than one hundred years. He loved creating new landscapes on the estate and dammed up a stream to develop an ornamental lake and family pleasure ground, which after 1900 became part of the Moigne Combe estate on the edge of the village (photo).

John Robert left £300 in his will for rebuilding the church, which had fallen into severe disrepair. It had to be completely rebuilt, starting in 1881, apart from the fourteenth-century tower which was repaired. It was finished two years later. His sister, Georgiana married Reverend George Stone of Devon. Their son, George John Stone, inherited the estate on the condition, once again in this family, that he changed his name to Cree, thus preserving the family name associated with the property. At that time, the estate included 29 separate properties and 1,285 acres of land. George John Cree enlarged Moignes Court, adding south and east wings and installing a staircase. The manor finally became a fine house. Not having been inhabited by its owners over the centuries, the court emerged from a rather simple hall of thirteenth century origin to a late Victorian house without passing through any intermediate stages. In 1893 George Cree had financial difficulties and initially secured loans from other members of the family, but later was forced to sell land to deal with the deficit.

Events of the Late Nineteenth Century

From 1875 there was a major collapse of British agriculture. After several poor seasons, cheap American grain imports and foodstuffs from all over the world flooded into Britain. The mass production of crops in the US Midwest on almost unlimited prairie lands, new railways carrying the grain to ports and new steamers transporting it across the Atlantic made life difficult for English farmers. Although agriculture was in fact better capitalised by this time, large estates found it increasingly difficult to turn a profit.

The Corn Laws had been passed in 1846. Disraeli, who opposed these, prophesied the ruin of agriculture as an inevitable consequence of free trade in grains. It took thirty years to prove him right. By the end of the century, the grain growing area in England had shrunk to less than six million acres. There was a corresponding fall in cattle and sheep prices, partly caused by new imports of frozen meat from Australia and New Zealand, following the invention of refrigerated ships. Enterprise gradually weakened and improvement such as drainage ceased. Land deteriorated in condition, and both owners and labourers struggled in an effort to make ends meet in the face of vanishing income.[1] Neither the Tories nor the Whigs supported agriculture or the needs of rural people. The Industrial Revolution and the people in the growing cities required cheap grain and other

---

[1] G.M. Trevelyan, Op. Cit, pp. 552-5.

foods. And the towns simply outvoted the country.

Emigration from Dorset did not start until the 1870s when rural wages began to improve slightly, providing some local people with the funds to move on. Initially artisans and labourers took advantage of work on the new roads and railways, earning their passage to the cities of the North. It was a time when many local girls left to go into service. There was a turnpike road which ran by the village from at least 1774, according to the local maps, making horse-drawn coaches and carriages a convenient mode of transport, but the journey even to Dorchester was a fairly long and arduous one.

While the railway from Dorchester to Southampton was completed in 1847, and the Great West Railway connected Salisbury to Weymouth in 1862, the flight from local poverty in those years was beyond the reach of most families. There were jobs in the industrial towns from 1840 onwards, but Dorset was once again in a deep agricultural depression. Without a subsidy for travel and relocation, such a move was as out of reach as Canada.[2] In 1880, the main crops of the village were recorded as wheat, oats, turnips and mangel wurzels, the latter grown for animal feed.

Local Government and Celebrations

The Local Government Act of 1888 established county councils which took over the activities previously held by the rural Justices of the Peace. Owermoigne had an elected

---

[2] Barbara Kerr, Op.Cit.

parish council from 1894. The last court case heard at Moignes Court was in 1902, after which all village disputes were heard in the county courts.

Moignes Court has been owned by six generations of the Cree family, who still occupy the house and own the surrounding land, now 550 acres. After the First World War the family sold the Old Forge and some of the properties in Moreton Road. The Westmacott post office and grocery remained a family enterprise until the 1950s. The family lost two sons in the First World War, as recorded on a commemorative plaque in the church. After the war, Miss Westmacott became the schoolmistress at the village school and lived in Chilbury Cottage, Pollards Lane, a residence traditionally reserved for schoolteachers. Today Westmacott remains an important name in the county, but no longer in the village. Apart from the Cree family, there are no village names listed in the records of a century ago to be found in the village today. Several of the old records include the Hardy family, doubtless part of the extended family of the author since his birthplace is a few miles away in Higher Bockhampton.

In 1897, the village had a great celebration for the Golden Jubilee of Queen Victoria. Following the ringing of the church bells, schoolchildren were awarded medals to mark the occasion and enjoyed a special tea, while the adults had a meal in the barn adjoining the church. The balance of the jubilee fund was spent on a handsome lamp and decorative ironwork erected over the entrance walk of St Michael's church, which remains a feature today.

The Twentieth Century and the Sale of the Village

The years before the First World War in the countryside have been often called "golden years" for the gentry and the wealthy middle class. They are reflected in the literature of the period. For others, things began to improve a little with the introduction of state pensions in 1909, the National Insurance Act of 1911 and the Health Insurance Act of 1912. But poverty and sickness still remained a serious problem for farmworkers and their families.

Horses were the undisputed masters of the highway. Dorset's 1,200 motoring pioneers prior to the First World War travelled a countryside which had neither a petrol station nor a tarmac road. The speed limit was 20mph and would remain so until the 1930s. Before the war, there were few tractors or wireless sets, no refrigerators or mains electricity. Houses were lit by paraffin lamps; water was drawn from the well and heated over the open fire. Most of the county's quarter of a million people lived, worked and died in the village of their forefathers. The school leaving age was 12 and an agricultural labourer's weekly wage was 12s 6d.[3]

During the First World War, cheap grain imports from America were curtailed by German ships in the Atlantic. Local grain production flourished once again, as the Germans attempted to starve Britain. Coastal defences had to be strengthened. The existing ones had been in place since the Napoleonic Wars one hundred years before. The demand for

---

[3] David Burnett, *A Dorset Camera 1914-1945*, Wimbourne: Dovecote Press, 1975, Introduction, n.p.

Church Lane circa 1920

Neighbours in the Moreton Road circa 1920

The Old Post Office and Shop

foodstuffs hastened mechanisation, which transformed farming quite rapidly. Villages like Owermoigne were much changed by the war and the years thereafter, as young men left to fight in the trenches and young women left to earn elsewhere. Only the older residents remained.

1926 was a very significant date for Owermoigne. In that year land and tied houses in the village were put up for sale by Cecil Cree. It was a historic transition. His decision may have been precipitated by the passage of the Rating and Valuation Act of the previous year, which established the first systematic taxation assessment system for properties and land. It may have been difficult to make ends meet on the estate, and an increase in an annual tax liability for the land and buildings may have influenced his decision to put the village on the market. The properties offered for sale included four farms, numerous smallholdings, thirty-eight enclosed pastures, the village school, ten "old world" cottages and eleven building sites (illustration).

The village history written collaboratively by members of the Women's Institute in 1983 used the auction notice for the 1926 sale of the village as their cover. They wrote that this date was of great significance to them, as it marked the passing from an old era to a new one. Several families who moved to the village at that time had jobs in nearby towns like Dorchester and Weymouth, but chose to live in a village location. Within twenty-five years, council houses were built on the main road and ten years after that two new bungalow estates followed which made housing available to the incomer population. The sale was the pivotal point in the transition from an old farming village to a new attractive location of cottages and bungalows which supported an entirely new group of people.

As late as 1929, there were still 13,000 cart horses in Dorset. And the county town of Dorchester continued to reflect both the old and new. A "servants' register" in South Street offered jobs as scullery maids and kitchen maids, while the town enjoyed its own somewhat erratic electricity supply. In the countryside there were new tarmac roads; houses were connected to the telephone and remote hamlets became more accessible.

In May 1936, Owermoigne celebrated the coronation of George VI with a series of holiday events including the planting of a commemorative tree, children's sports events, a tea and a cricket match. In the evening there was a communal listening to the first empire broadcast by the king followed by a toast, community singing, a torchlight procession, bonfire, fireworks and dance. Tickets were 1s for adults and 6d for children.[1]

The Village Hall and Changes in Agriculture

The Owermoigne village hall was built in 1937, when Cecil Cree donated a plot of land to the village; it was built by subscription and voluntary labour. From then on village dances and events were held often, and village residents were able to hire the hall for private functions. The following year there was a wedding party, football dance, children's party and a Conservative social meeting. A piano was obtained in

---

[1] Owermoigne Women's Institute, Op.Cit, n.p.

1939 and the hall hosted another dance and wedding that year.[2]

Dorset had become very well known nationally and internationally by this time, thanks to the popularity of Hardy's novels. The Hardy Players were founded in the 1920s, late in his life yet at the height of his national acclaim. While the small troupe occasionally travelled to London, they mainly performed dramatisations of the author's plays locally. The last remaining member of the Hardy Players was Norrie Woodall who came to live in Owermoigne in 1938 where she established a chicken farm with her father.

During the Thirties, the Forestry Commission was set up, the Ramblers Association founded and Ordnance Survey maps became widely available. Successive governments began to legislate to protect one of its greatest national assets, the countryside. Bournemouth grew from a fishing village in the late nineteenth century to a major town, hosting 55,000 visitors on the summer bank holiday in 1939. Weymouth, made popular by seaside visits since George III holidayed there a century before, preserved its Regency architecture and grew substantially. Poole and Lyme Regis were also popular seaside destinations. And small villages like Lulworth Cove, a few miles from the Owermoigne, served as examples of bucolic seaside England for city dwellers. The AA and RAC gave motorists information on rural itineraries and the first Shell Guide to Dorset was published in 1938.

---

[2] Owermoigne Women's Institute Ibid.

Traditional rural industries such as hurdle-making, weaving, potting, dry-stone walling, thatching and quilting were threatened by new technologies and urban-made products. The village blacksmith was challenged by the need to meet changes in the local market and adopt modern methods. Many local blacksmiths became local garages in the Thirties or after the war, as was the case of the Olds family of West Stafford. The blacksmith's son, Peter Olds, later became one of the most successful entrepreneurs in the county with a chain of car dealerships. He built a multi-million pound country mansion on the edge of Owermoigne a few years ago. The village smithy was located some distance from the main road and was therefore not suitable to become a garage. The blacksmith retired and the Old Forge became a tearoom.

A rural industries bureau tried to assist local craftsmen, especially women, to diversify their activities, but by the Thirties few rural crafts were left in the village. The shop and post office were busy, as few people had access to private transport and public transport was still rudimentary.

Local dairy and poultry farming, as well as livestock rearing, were reasonably successful, while cereal farming declined throughout the country. In 1931 a series of quotas and tariffs began protecting agricultural production. At the same time, the government encouraged farmers to increase productivity through land drainage, soil improvement and mechanisation. In 1938, there were only 4,000 tractors in the whole of England, mostly on farms of upwards of 300 acres. Rural wages remained low – around one third of an urban job – and conditions were still poor. Almost half the parishes in England lacked a sewerage system and had only rudimentary piped water. Inside picturesque whitewashed thatched cottages, there was still no electricity, earth floors and miserable poverty.[3] New rural housing became a national priority.

Between 1919 and 1939, 800,000 new homes were built in rural England, although Owermoigne had to wait until 1949 to have its first council houses. In southeast England rapid bungalow development spread to the suburbs and rural villages housing people from towns and cities.[4] Dorset was too remote to experience this. It remained a long slow rail journey to any large city. The Health, Pension and Insurance Acts, which were passed in 1911, were extended in the Thirties, thus consolidating the early welfare state. By this time most homes had a wireless to listen to the BBC. The market town of Wareham opened its first cinema in 1929, and organisations such as the Women's Institute and the Young Farmers, encouraged people to meet to discuss common issues. The development of both acreage subsidies for barley and oats and marketing boards for milk and bacon helped the gradual climb out of the depression of the Thirties.

The Second World War

"On 2 August 1940, people living along the south coast looked out their windows to find that the previous night had brought a shower of leaflets – 'The Last Appeal to Reason by Adolph Hitler.' Delighted households collected this German

---

[3] Juliet Gardiner, *The Thirties: An Intimate Portrait*, London: Harper Press, 2010, p.242.
[4] Gardiner Ibid.

propaganda. Some threaded them on loops of string and hung them over the privy door for use as lavatory paper...."[5] Dorset had become frontline Britain after the fall of Dunkirk. Three hundred pillboxes were built along the coast, as well as tank barriers and machine gun trenches, to deter infantry landings. After the Channel Islands were invaded in the summer, the Luftwaffe turned its attention to Weymouth, an important naval base since Henry VIII. It also was a submarine base and had two torpedo factories for the war effort. The town was dive bombed many times and suffered extensive night bombing as the people huddled in air raid shelters. By September 1940 some respite arrived as the German air bombardment switched its activities to London and other cities.

Starting in September 1939, 1.5 million children had been evacuated from London and other major cities. They came mainly from inner city slums, and most enjoyed their relative freedom in the villages of Dorset and other rural counties. Householders were paid 8s 6d for each child – a welcome earner for host families.[6] But the children were not always welcome: in May 1941, Albert Bulley, who had a bungalow in the village, was fined £5 for refusing to accept evacuee children.

The events of the war remained dramatic for some years. The RAF established Warmwell airfield which became critical during the Battle of Britain as a base for Hurricanes and

---

[5] Juliet Gardiner, *Wartime Britain, 1939-1945*, London: Headline Press, 2004, pp. 260-61.
[6] Gardiner Ibid, p.36.

Spitfires. It was a few miles from the village, on the site where the village football team now play home games. Flying combat missions was not considered a job for anyone over thirty. Many were recruited from public schools and became known as the "Brylcreem Boys".[7]

There were a couple of gun emplacements along the coast and a wire stretching from White Nothe to Portland for the detection of submarines. There were aerial dogfights every day in the early war years all over the area and several German planes were shot down. An RAF pilot bailed out over Watercombe Farm on 7 October, 1940, having been hit by a Messerschmitt over Weymouth. It was too low for his parachute to open and he was killed. The same day two German airman bailed out unhurt nearby. The next day, Moreton church was hit by a German Stuka bomb meant for Warmwell airfield.[8]

On one occasion a few German troops landed successfully. A few police turned up and told them to take off their shoes, knowing that the only escape was across burned maize stubble in the field which would be highly uncomfortable. Then they called for reinforcements to gather them up. For a while the planes went over every night about 7pm, people living in Holworth reported. They said it was almost possible to set your watch by them. The planes were on their way to bomb Bristol or the Midland cities. Occasionally they would

---

[7] Gardiner Ibid, p.276.
[8] Rebuilt by local subscription after the war, the stained glass windows which were blown out were replaced by Laurence Whistler etched glass providing exceptional light. It is the finest collection of his work in a single place.

jettison their bombs along the coast. After the war there was a great deal of debris all around, including a German fighter plane which lay there for a long time. Richard, whose family had a cottage overlooking the sea in Holworth, reported that one afternoon a Luftwaffe pilot trailing his parachute climbed over the wall and joined us for tea. He looked for all the world like a local rambler and spoke very good English. After tea, they called the police.

In July 1940 the Ministry of Information together with the War Office issued a leaflet entitled "Beating the Invader" which was distributed to people in the area. It advised that:

> *...although along our coasts, the greater part will remain unaffected. But where the enemy lands, or tries to land, there will be most violent fighting. Not only will there be battles when the enemy tries to come ashore, but afterwards there will fall upon his lodgements very heavy British counter-attacks...So if you are advised to leave the place where you live, it is your duty to go elsewhere when you are told to leave. You will have to get to the safest place you can find and stay there until the battle is over. For all of you then the order and duty will be: STAND FIRM.*

How to "CARRY ON", in further precise detail, was also provided. The order was signed by Winston Churchill. It caused considerable local concern as it brought home the seriousness of the situation.[9] Children initially evacuated to

---

[9] Rodney Legg, *Wartime Dorset: The Complete History*, Wincanton, Dorset Publishing, 2000, pp. 48-49.

coastal areas like Dorset were moved to inland locations during this period.

Polish pilots were also based at RAF Warmwell from 1941, and from 1944 they were joined by American Air Force crews and bombers in preparation for D-Day. From 1940, the airfield was frequently bombed. Bovington army base, a few miles north of the village, had been established before World War I as the headquarters of the Royal Armoured Corps. Established as a tank base after they were developed in 1914, its ranks swelled with thousands of recruits from all over the country by 1940. The Armoured Fighting Vehicles School of Gunnery was also established at Lulworth. Both remain in operation today.

Radar was invented and developed between 1940 and 1942, at nearby Worth Matravers. About 200 people worked there, most billeted with local families. This gave rise to many local stories of the brilliant scientists and boffins on the project living with local village families. Worth was chosen because of the flat cliff-top site. Radar could be said to have been the single most critical invention which protected the coastline of Britain and helped win the war.

After twenty years of peace and cheap imports between the wars, British farms had been almost entirely given over to pastures. The government targeted 1.7 million acres for food crops in 1940. In blackout conditions, farmers often worked round the clock with tractors and horses. The target was met.[10] The Land Army was the solution to the manpower

---

[10] Rodney Legg, Op. Cit, p. 140.

needed on the farms. There were Land Girls volunteering from big cities, serving as they had during the Great War. The government wanted to make the country as self-sufficient as possible since the Atlantic shipping lanes were so vulnerable. More and more people were needed to work on the land. The shortfall was eventually met by prisoners-of-war, mostly Italians. At Watercombe Farm there were two German prisoners-of-war working as farm hands, described by Margaret, who grew up in the village during the war, as "rather snazzy".

A "ploughing-up" campaign turned grassland over to grow wheat, oats, barley and potatoes. Sheep were encouraged over beef cattle as they did not depend on imported feed. The Ministry of Agriculture controlled food production and prices. Unproductive land was brought into cultivation and tractors and threshing machines gradually replaced lingering horse-drawn equipment. Helped by the extensive use of fertilisers, food production rose 91 per cent during the war and Britain was able to feed itself for 160 days of the year rather than 120 when the war broke out.[11]

War Memories in Owermoigne and Tyneham

Norrie Woodall, a young member of the Hardy Players during the life of the poet and author, died in 2011 at the age of 105. She wrote a memoir about wartime Owermoigne. Her poultry farm on the edge of the village supplied the officer's mess at Warmwell airfield with eggs. But as the war

---

[11] Rodney Legg Ibid, p. 141.

progressed, she found it difficult to find enough feed for the chickens. She was ordered by the county War Agricultural Executive Committee to plough up two acres of land in order to plant potatoes. The farm was so near the airfield that Norrie's family often had to use their shelter and was sometimes called upon to house several airmen overnight because of the danger of delayed explosive action at the airfield.

Unlike city dwellers in ration queues, village people had plenty of eggs, milk, ham and bacon. Milking was still done by hand, often by older children. Local men hunted for rabbits, pigeons, pheasants and other birds to supplement war rations. Despite the long hours, the farmers felt for the first time perhaps that they were more valued by the rest of the country for their efforts. Prices for food remained high throughout the war. From 1940, Owermoigne village hall was used for army lectures and sometimes for billeting troops.

In preparation for the eventual landing on the coast of France, the nearby village of Tyneham was commandeered by the army in December 1943, and civilians were evacuated to enable the soldiers to do practice manoeuvres in landing craft at nearby Worbarrow Bay. Dorset was selected for practice manoeuvres as it had a coastline very similar to the Normandy beaches. Many lives were lost in these landing exercises owing to storms and local currents. Major-General Mark Bond, who has lived at Moigne Combe on the outskirts of the village since the war, was the son of the family who owned the manor house in Tyneham and most of the surrounding farm land.

Army activity left Tyneham in a sorry state. The crofters'

cottages along the coast and the houses of the entire village, a mile inland, were destroyed. When the people of Tyneham left in 1943, they nailed a notice to the church door – only one of two structures which survived the army activity. It declared their faith in the cause of king and country for which they were pleased to leave their homes. And it implored the incoming army to look after the village. Unfortunately after the war, despite many representations to Parliament and Downing Street, the Ministry of Defence retained the entire site, which today forms part of the Lulworth tank training base. Major-General Bond, as a member of the leading family of the village, campaigned with the local people despite his doubtless divided loyalty as a serving officer during and after the war.[12]

D-Day

The American entry into the war brought thousands of troops to Dorset. On D-Day 30,000 US troops left for Normandy from Weymouth Harbour. Along the Dorset coast at Studland, Churchill, Eisenhower and Montgomery watched the invasion fleet leave for the French coast. "Liberty ships" had been put into service by the American government to bring much needed food and other supplies to Britain throughout the war. Several hundred were lost to U-boat attacks or fire and storm damage, leaving wrecks which still lie off the Dorset coast, adding to the hundreds of ships which had been sunk along the coast in the previous centuries. Following the war these became of interest to local amateur

---

[12] Patrick Wright, *The Village that Died for England: The Strange Story of Tyneham*, London: Jonathan Cape, 1995.

divers.

During the conflict, the village Air Raid Precaution (ARP) headquarters in Owermoigne was in Church Lane. Village warnings locally were often given with a hand whistle, and the all clear with a handbell. Norrie Woodall was charged with communication between Owermoigne and Crossways, then a hamlet near RAF Warmwell. Mostly done by telephone, she occasionally had to drive with no headlights to find the warden of Crossways, who was usually in his shelter. The noise of the aircraft was almost deafening, she reported.

One night there was a crump and a bomb which shook Norrie's house. The ARP duty warden in the village phoned to ask if she was all right and then asked her to go outside to see if she could see anything! There was nothing, but the next day, it was announced that a farmer had been killed across the fields from her house. While there was a Home Guard in the village, they were woefully unprepared for battle, with only one rifle between them. Norrie remembers the intense roar of planes for hours on end in early June 1944, the start of the invasion to liberate Europe.[13]

---

[13] A.N. Woodall, "Owermoigne Remembered," unpub., n.p.

Chapter Three

Wartime Memories and After

Arthur

The telephone rings as we sit in the front garden of Arthur's house on a fine day at the end of June 2009. "Ah, that is our French granddaughter," Arthur says. "She is coming to visit. Since the fiftieth anniversary of D-Day in 1994, I have stayed with her grandfather in Normandy every year in June. He had served in the French Air Force and was captured during the German invasion. He specifically asked to have pilots from the Glider Pilot Regiment as his guests on the D-Day commemoration. Guy spoke no English and I, no French, but with a strong will to communicate, lots of gestures, drawings and notes, we became friends. Claire was devoted to her grandfather. When he died several years later, she said to me 'You are now my grandfather.' We were at her wedding a few years ago when she announced that she was expecting a baby boy who would be called Arthur. I was so surprised and moved. They visit us every year."

Arthur has lived in the village since 1997, when he married Margaret. Following military service, he married and was living in Bournemouth working as a van driver. They first met when Margaret was sixteen and working in Weymouth after the war. She cycled every day from the village, a distance of eleven miles, as there was no public transport. Arthur regularly delivered supplies to her firm and one day he offered her a lift home in the van with her bike. They became close friends and Arthur was often invited to tea in the village with Margaret's mother. Arthur was already married. They kept in touch after Margaret married and they both raised families (including emigration to Canada for Margaret and the family for eight years). Their relationship finally blossomed when their respective spouses died in the 1990s: a love story spanning fifty years.

Arthur is Irish by background which perhaps accounts for his considerable talent as a storyteller. His family came from Mayo during the famine in the mid-nineteenth century and settled in various towns in Yorkshire. Arthur and his family lived just outside Halifax in an isolated river valley, a village called Shipden. His father was a millwright who maintained the equipment in the local woollen mills. Arthur was very bright at school and had been offered a place in the local grammar school, but his headmaster informed him that although he could obtain a grant for books and uniform, he might well feel out of place in the middle-class preserve of a grammar school since he was from a poor family.
In the 1920s it was often difficult for poor children to thus get ahead and join the meritocracy. Arthur's mother was very keen for him to take up the place, but his father endorsed the view of the headmaster. He left school at 14 and regrets the decision to this day. Arthur applied for his first job as an apprentice grocer in the co-op movement which was paid better than the other jobs on offer. He did not make it first time round and worked for a while as a creeler in the weaving shed of the mills, looking after the looms. With large contracts for seat upholstery for the railway companies the factory was working full tilt.

Arthur was 21 in 1939 when he was drafted into National

Service. Although the war had not begun, it was looming when he started his six months' army training. The new recruits were given leave to help with the harvest that year. He was delivering milk from a cart when one of the neighbours invited him in to hear Chamberlain's broadcast declaring war. Arthur was given his orders in October and went to Blackdown railway station where he would receive a ticket to wherever it said on the call-up notice. The booking clerk was chewing on a pencil, he recalled, as he asked where he was to go. When he said "Aldershot", Arthur asked him where that was. He had never been beyond Scarborough and his knees went weak when he learned it was in southeast England, not far from London. Together with two mates, they went to London and braved the Circle Line to try to get to Waterloo. After passing though Kings Cross for the second time, they knew were in need of assistance. At Waterloo they were directed to the Union Jack Club where they enjoyed an excellent three-course meal for 9d. People they met kept saying, "Bloody good luck to you." After a while it began to seem to him more than a bit ominous.

At Aldershot, they joined the Royal Horse Artillery. The uniform included riding britches, puttees (gaiters) and spurs. It was perilous going down stairs with spurs and the puttees unravelled if you did not do them very carefully. In the first parade, the sergeant major asked if anyone had "equine" skills. No one volunteered. Then he said "Come on. You lads from Yorkshire must have ridden horses before now." Understanding was achieved and several volunteered. But there were no horses so they were assigned to mules, which the lads found rather tedious.

They had gun drills without guns. There was very little equipment so in a complex mime, they went through the motions of loading the shells, moving the guns, etc. Bizarre though it was, they learned how to do it by the time the guns became available. In January 1940, Arthur and the others were sent to a base in Derbyshire. The guns finally arrived a month later. His new regiment was Motor Transport, the 54th and he became a dispatch rider. In March that year he was sent to Castleton in Derbyshire and learned to ride a motorbike in the Peak District. He naturally preferred riding his bike to parades and the rest of army drill. On the motorbike on dispatch, he was out on his own most of the time which would have suited any young soldier. He was then put in charge of the regimental bikes and got his first stripe and a 9d a day raise.

In May 1940 they were in Bristol awaiting departure to France. They were detailed to help the retreating troops from Dunkirk settle back into their regiments. They then served in the local area on the South Coast which had gun emplacements from Bognor to Lyme waiting for the invasion. There were many air raids and severe bombings. Arthur had to go to a naval installation at Portsmouth with a dispatch. As he entered the base on his bike, he heard someone yelling and screaming and running towards him. A cadet told him that he had just ridden across the quarterdeck. He looked back confused when the sailor shouted "Nelson's quarterdeck – where he was killed". Arthur replied that he thought he had been killed at sea. His ignorance of navy matters thus exposed, the sailor explained (with restored patience and calm) that every naval installation on land or at sea has a quarterdeck in his honour. Such things are not forgotten.

Arthur as a soldier and son

Arthur at Arnhem

Arthur watched the Battle of Britain for the next few months from army positions on the South Coast, the dog-fights in the air and the shrapnel falling. He witnessed a sordid incident when a German plane came down. The four crew were clearly dead. Up rolled a local police van to oversee the incident and they helped themselves to the watches of the four airmen. When he told them such an act was wrong, they said, "What difference does it make? They are dead." He was deeply shocked. Later when he saw his first dead German near Arnhem, he felt that he could still not hate him, but several hours later when one of his close mates was killed his mood changed. He had learned to hate.

In early 1942, Arthur's unit was still in Britain. He did map reading for a major who could not read maps. With his friend Henry, a gunnery officer, they began looking for possibilities to move on to something more exciting and better paid. Henry kept coming up with ideas like a parachute regiment or the Commandos, but the major always vetoed these as he did not want to lose them.

The Glider Pilot Regiment (GPR) finally became their escape. The regiment was a War Office priority and thus they were at last able to get around the major's veto. In May 1942 they joined the GPR. There was a rigorous selection process for four days and extensive interviews. "They seemed to be looking for supermen who could do everything – take the initiative and be flexible," Arthur reflected. The selection included training and intelligence tests. Once passed, they did pilot training on power craft including multi engine aircraft first, then gliders. The gliders were towed by bombers almost to their destination carrying troops and equipment. Once landed the glider pilots became infantry, sappers or whatever regiment they had transported. The gliders carried jeeps, small tanks and artillery. In June 1944, three gliders from the GPR (each carrying 30 men) landed near Pegasus Bridge behind the enemy lines in preparation for D-Day. The river crossing was crucial to the Allied troops moving inland once they had left the beaches. The action was a success, but at a considerable loss of life, including fifty glider pilots. Arthur lost several close friends. He returns every year on the anniversary of the D-Day invasion and pays his respects to these fallen comrades.

The annual celebrations always start with a dinner at the café at Pegasus Bridge, still owned by the family which had been there during the action in 1945. The father of the present owner had buried the stock of champagne when the Germans invaded the area to be restored when the British took the bridge in 1944. The visit continues to the local cemetery where Arthur's comrades are buried, alongside the first British soldier to lose his life on the eve of D-Day. Their bodies were never removed to the nearby British war grave cemetery, at the request of the local people.

On Sunday 17 September, 1944 Arthur landed near Arnhem in the Netherlands. "Operation Market Garden" was Montgomery's strategic plan to destroy the German anti-aircraft guns which would have made Allied flights to Germany much safer. Had it succeeded, it might have shortened the war by six months. But things fell apart in the operation of the mission and it was a disaster. The GPR gliders came over on three successive days. Arthur remembers, "Ours landed near a Dutch farmhouse. The first thing which put us on alert was a German soldier coming out of a barn. We noticed he was doing up his trousers: his braces were hanging down. When he saw us, he began shaking. We gestured to him to pull up his braces, as if he'd put his hands up his trousers would have fallen down. We gave him a cigarette and saw a Dutch lass coming out of the barn doing up her dress. That was our introduction to the enemy!"

While the parachute regiments were landing, Arthur recounts, "I noticed a very full cow and milked it. The frothy warm milk was wonderful, but my London colleagues were disgusted and would not share it. The Germans were all over the woods shelling and we could not get to Arnhem. We only made it as far as the outskirts. We were sent three miles back to the Hartenstein Hotel which had become Allied headquarters for the operation. I hated trenches – digging them or being in them, as I had a fear of being suffocated. The "stonk" [shelling] continued fiercely. I was hit in the shoulder and fell into the canal, a bullet which is still lodged in my bone. I was picked up by Canadian sappers who had motorised rubber boats on the canal. Then the boat itself was blown up and I was hit by shrapnel. But the water was very cold and it numbed the pain. I was floating along wondering where my body would be washed out. Rotterdam? Amsterdam? Or would I be caught in the weeds and left to rot? These are the strange things which come to mind when you think your time has come."

Arthur heard a voice say, "Give us a hand with this body." And I shouted, 'I am not a body!' I was carried into a building on the other side of the canal, which was a first aid post. I was transferred to the hospital at Nijmegen. We were taken by convoy through German lines to an airfield which took us to Brussels. We landed in Gloucestershire at the end of September." The regiment lost 365 glider pilots at Arnhem.

Following his time in casualty, Arthur had two weeks leave in Bournemouth with his wife and young son after which he was re-posted near Salisbury: "I persuaded them to let me retain my A1 status so I could go on another mission. I wanted to get back to my squadron or what was left of it. But they said this might not be possible. I found myself in an empty tent for a while. Then some new glider pilot recruits arrived and I learned that they were about to be shipped out, so I just hung along with them and eventually made it back to active service."

The next mission was to land across the Rhine in March 1945 and raise hell making the way safe for the Allied armies based on the other side. They were ordered to land the gliders alongside the parachute drop and kill as many Germans as they could. The gliders flew in under heavy fire: many were blown out of the air. Arthur heard a thud and could not turn the rudder, his navigator informed him that some of the wing had blown off and a hit at the rear had immobilised the steering. They landed safely about 10.30am and by 3 o'clock that afternoon, the Allied sappers were building the pontoon bridges across the Rhine. In all, 120 were killed of the 800 who landed. The war was in its final phase.

Arthur was sent to the American airbase at Greenham Common after that. He recalls it as paradise: tents with wooden flooring, beds with sheets, all the cigarettes and candy you could consume together with other goodies in the PX. "This is the life," we thought. Even the mess was excellent. They were waiting for clearance for a mission to fly the gliders to Paris – the Champs Elysées no less, carrying

American Rangers whom it was planned would punch out the Perspex windows on the gliders and shoot up the Germans on either side of the street. News was announced by tannoy every day and the mission was postponed for several weeks. It was eventually cancelled when Paris was declared an open city by the German Commandant. "Thank God, we all thought, as the American inspired action seemed more than a bit balmy to us. I sometimes think when I reflect on all this that we didn't win the war. The Germans lost it."

The Glider Pilot Regiment became part of the Army Air Corps in 1957. Several times a year Arthur joins them for dinners and has often addressed the trainees on the base: "I tell the story of the German and his braces. But perhaps most importantly, I have every year revisited Normandy and Arnhem to pay my respects to fallen comrades. We have formed a Glider Pilot Brotherhood, although there are now not many of us left." The veterans attend an annual reunion which in recent years has been organised by Arthur and Margaret in Bournemouth.

In June 2013 the annual visit to Pegasus Bridge included about 30 people, eight of Arthur's generation. At the Bridge Café the woman of the house always tells the same story about her father hiding the champagne from the Germans and maintains the fiction each year that the bottles still come from that cache. Arthur's annual calendar includes the anniversary celebrations of D-Day and the battles of Arnhem and the Rhine. In September 2013 Arthur and Margaret attended the dedication of the Glider Pilot Regiment memorial stone at the National Arboretum in Staffordshire. The stone was granite, quarried just outside Arnhem, a gift of the Dutch government.

Arthur attends the "Not Forgotten" days at the Army Air Corps base in Wiltshire and the Armistice celebrations. A book on the battle of Arnhem was published a few years ago with twenty-five references to Arthur together with the photo of him in uniform with his son on his lap. Arthur is now 95 years old but still plants an annual crop of vegetables with the help of his wife, Margaret. He is very sociable and many people in the village have learned of his fantastic recall of his wartime activities. He read Tennyson's "Crossing the Bar" at the Thanksgiving Service for my husband, Donal, in St Michael's Church in August 2012.

Margaret

Margaret was born in Dairy Cottage in 1933. Her father did hedges and ditches around the village and played the concertina at village hall events. They were moved by Dorset council when she was very young to a timber cottage with a large veranda on the main road. With siblings and other young friends, she used to earn a ha'penny opening the gates to the Holworth Road. Despite being very poor, Margaret always described her childhood in the village as a happy one, particularly enjoying the company of other children. But life was not easy. "Our poverty did us no harm at all," she said. I learned thrift watching my mother scrape together money for the rent and great respect for her efforts.

Margaret's father died when she was eight; her mother had taken in washing to make ends meet even prior to that time. Margaret remembers collecting the washing for her mother in a bundle. A large vat would be boiled on the fire in the yard and her mother worked it round with a large stick.

Hung out to dry in the yard, it was then ironed with a flat iron heated on the paraffin stove. Margaret had to distribute the neat piles of ironing (sheets on the bottom to hankies on top) to people in the village which she found rather humiliating. At least with the bundle of dirty laundry slung over her shoulder no one knew what she was carrying. Margaret remembers that the families whose washing her mother did were not rich; some of them lived in Charity Cottages.

During the war, Margaret and her friends used to go up on the downs between the village and the coast. They sometimes collected silver tape caught on the bushes, unaware of what it was. It had been placed there to confuse German fighter aircraft flying towards the coast by intercepting their radar. She and her friends felt free to roam with a small band of children. They had no fear. She loved the village school, attending from the age of two. There were about twenty children in the one-room school. The teacher was Miss Westmacott whose two brothers were killed during the war, commemorated on a plaque in the church. Margaret also lost a brother during the war, clearing mines from the Kiel Canal in North Germany.

Margaret, recognised as a particularly bright pupil, was encouraged to take the scholarship exam early. She won a place at the Green School, the girl's grammar school in Dorchester when she was ten in 1944. The grant money for her uniform did not arrive in time for the start of term. Her mother made her a uniform and coat from an older sister's clothing, but it was purple and did not match the others. She felt humiliated. It was a bad start. She found her fellow students "starchy". It felt radically different to the free and unfettered life she had in the village. In principle the scholarship system was created to encourage bright children of working-class origin to go to grammar schools. But money was required for books and uniforms. Sometimes even these were offered by school heads. Margaret recounts how she hated the social life at the Green School because she "felt different" as a working man's daughter.

Margaret left the Green School as soon as she could at 14 and went to Leeds to stay with her sister, as her mother was in a sanatorium with TB. There she trained as a comptometer operator – an early calculator. Returning to Dorset when her mother was restored to health, she got the job in Weymouth.

Margaret and her first husband, who worked at the nearby Galton Nursery and as a local gardener, did not have a place to live and emigrated to Canada on a £10 assisted passage. She described the time in Toronto as "very lonely". She had her first two children there. After eight years they returned to Dorset. Her mother died and she and her husband were allocated a council house in the village. When she and Arthur were married they remained in the same house in Kit Lance near the entrance to the village. They are among the few residents who remain council tenants. On principle, they wish the property to remain as social housing. Margaret worked in the West Dorset District Council as an accounts officer for six years; then as an officer in the housing department dealing with homeless families. She was thus aware of the great need to retain the social housing stock. She is always an avowed supporter of the underdog (her term), which she feels is explained by the poverty in her background. She hates social injustice.

Margaret and Arthur have been retired for many years, but until this year have always done contract work for the council distributing polling cards and information. They have a large vegetable and flower garden and a stall in front of the house selling alstroemeria, gladioli and sweet peas in the summer months. They travel together annually to the Second World War commemoration events and have many children and grandchildren. Margaret has served on the parish council for years.

Edna

From south London, the newly married, Edna and her husband moved to Dorset in 1940 when he was drafted into military service at the Royal Tank Division base at Bovington, about four miles from the village. The base, established after the first World War, was the posting and final home of T.E. Laurence, whose small crude crofter's cottage is at Clouds Hill, just outside the perimeter of the base. It is now owned by the National Trust and receives a large number of visitors from home and abroad each year. They take turns crowding into the tiny dwelling to listen to the local guides, all of whom are ardent admirers of Lawrence. Edna had an office job on the base. On the eve of being shipped out to the Middle East, Edna's husband was made a training commander and remained in Dorset for the war. She considered herself a very lucky war bride.

After the war, they moved to Winfrith. Things were buzzing because the Atomic Energy Authority had set up a reactor and research installation nearby. The tenant at the Red Lion pub on the main road, who had been there since before the First World War, wanted to retire. He recommended Edna's husband to the tenancy and they took it over – including rats and cockroaches but a fine new thatched roof. They remained tenants at the Red Lion for thirty years and raised a family there. Their eldest son, Michael, took it over afterwards and ran it for a further fifteen years. When the caravan holiday park in Owermoigne came on the market, Michael bought it and moved Edna and her husband to an adjoining house once they had retired.

Before her death in 2010 at 85, Edna sat reading from her comfortable chair, her favourite pastime, among photos of her children, grandchildren and great grandchildren. The grandchildren had become doctors and barristers and she was very proud of them. She had daily carers and enjoyed a spectacular view over farmland at the rear of a very light and airy house. She liked to get to activities in the village when she could get a lift. She often thought that it would have been nicer to live in the middle of the village rather than nearly a mile away so she could see people more often.

Major-General Mark Bond

The wartime story of the Dorset village of Tyneham is known as "the village that died for England".[1] The entire village was commandeered in 1943 as a training location for the D-Day landings. It was a mile from the beach at Warbarrow Bay and the situation and geography were quite similar to the Normandy villages the Allies would invade two years later.

---

[1] Patrick Wright, *The Village that Died for England: The Strange Story of Tyneham,* London, Jonathan Cape, 1995.

Mark Bond was the eldest son of the Bond family who had owned the manor house in the village since 1683. They held seventy acres of mixed farmland in the beautiful surrounding area at the time of the enforced evacuation. Mark attended Eton as had his father and grandfather. He was in the army in 1943. He served first in Egypt, where he was wounded, and subsequently in the Italian campaign, when he was wounded again and captured by the Germans. He was liberated in April 1945 by the American forces. After the war he served in the army on the Rhine and taught at the Imperial War College in London. Eventually reaching the rank of major-general, he served as Assistant Chief of the Defense Staff in Hong Kong and a Planning Officer at the Ministry of Defence.

His parents moved to Moigne Combe during the wartime evacuation, a property on the edge of Owermoigne owned by his great uncle. It is on land which had previously been owned by the Cree family, who set up a pleasure garden, lake and summer house in the nineteenth century. The house is Edwardian, built by H. Pomeroy Bond, JP in 1900 with a fine garden and sixty-five acres of woodland.

Departing soldiers pinned notes to the church door declaring that they were happy to do their duty for king and country, but asked the army to look after the village in their absence. They always expected to return. After the war the people of the village formed the Tyneham Action Group to petition Parliament, Downing Street and the MoD to allow them to return, rebuild the village and re-establish their homes. By then the army had installed a gunnery school on an adjacent site and was using the hills surrounding the village for tank manoeuvres. Bond was drawn to support the Tyneham Action Group and became its chair when he retired from the army. He felt that the group "was sensible and composed of sincere and reasonable people with practical and reasonable aims."[2] He felt that the army could have reduced the size of the shooting ranges to their prewar dimensions, thus allowing people to return to the village. But the campaign fell on deaf ears in London. In the postwar period, the Ministry of Defence and the army were in the ascendant and influential in government decisions. With the onset of the Korean conflict and the looming Cold War, successive governments consistently ignored the case of the Tyneham villagers about their return. When the group split into two factions, Bond resigned as chair believing that there was no more he could do.

When he returned to civilian life in 1970, Major-General Bond became the chair of the Wareham Magistrates' Court and chair of the Police Authority. He also served on Dorset County Council for twenty years, twelve as chair and as the Vice Lord-Lieutenant and High Sheriff. Bond was also a founder member of the Dorset Wildlife Trust and the Dorset Archaeological Society and a governor of Milton Abbey School. He joined with other local landowners and residents to save the Purbeck coastline from development, which was respected by the local authority and remains a spectacular natural asset including the World Heritage Site of the Jurassic Coast. On the Moigne Combe estate, which includes twenty acres of heath and 160 acres of tenanted farmland, he planted 65,000 trees.

---

[2] Ibid.

Cecily

Until the age of 92 Cecily was Major-General Bond's housekeeper, having been in post for 28 years. Her father had been born in Tyneham, but came to live at Galton, a nearby farm when he was young. It was there that she grew up. She had happy memories of Galton as a child and described her family, named Ricketts, as "God fearing, doing charity and not quarrelling". Her brother William, who started work on the farm when he was 14, used to say, "We have not many worldly possessions, but mother will always be at the gate."

She cycled to Moreton station and attended the Green School in Dorchester. On her grandmother's side, the family owned the mill in Owermoigne at the time. Cecily's grandmother lived opposite the church and raised eleven children. She had trained as a midwife and district nurse and walked the parish doing her round of house visits. Her grandfather was a coachman to the Cree family and appears in a family photograph with a top hat taken at the pleasure garden at Moigne Combe. Cecily married and lived near Moreton Station with her husband, returning to Galton during the war to live with her mother while her husband was on active service.

Prior to the construction of the village hall, she remembered that a barn near the church was used for local events. She talked of social evenings, amateur dramatics and dancing. Cecily's husband was a founding member of the Owermoigne Football Club and played for them in the Thirties. Some years ago, she sent a donation and words of encouragement to the team which were reprinted in the parish magazine: "Do it again lads!, hard work, determination and above all team work, no hugging the ball for the individual goal..." It was greatly appreciated.

Elizabeth

Elizabeth was married to Cecily's brother, Will, who worked throughout his life on the farm at Galton from the age of fourteen to seventy. She was born in the Kennington Road in London, a mile south of Westminster Bridge. As a young person, she described the freedom of travelling around London to Regents Park and South Kensington to the museums. She recalled the companionship of her older sister who read them stories as children and later became a Methodist lay preacher.

Elizabeth's mother was ill prior to the war and the children were dispersed to children's homes. She and her sister were sent to Bournemouth where they lived for three years from the age of twelve. They slept in dormitories and had a playroom for games. There were people to read to them, but she longed for a proper family life again. Her other sisters were in Devon and her brother in Wales. At 15 she had to leave the children's home and was sent back to London. It was 1941!

During the Blitz they could hear the doodlebug bombs overhead. Their Baptist church had been bombed, so they attended the Congregational church. Elizabeth joined the Girls' Fire Brigade and watched the Air Raid Precautions organisation pulling people out of a nearby house. Her father worked for London Underground and was therefore exempt from military service. At night he did a fire watch all along the tube tunnels.

Elizabeth joined the Land Army at the age of 17 and was sent to Wimborne in Dorset to a hostel. After a year she applied for work on the farm at Moignes Court, where she was housed in Dairy Cottage in Church Lane with another girl. At 5am every day they would gather in the cows and milk them, in winter with torches. She milked about fifteen cows each day after which she turned the hay and did other farm chores. She met Will, her future husband, while working as a Land Girl. He used to come from Galton to help out at the weekends. They were married in 1948 and settled into a tied cottage at Galton where Will continued to work.

They lived at Galton all their working lives attending church in Owermoigne. Will's aged mother lived at Galton with his brother, Tony, also worked on the farm. Elizabeth organised the flower arrangements in the church in the village. The farm at Galton was purchased in 1978 by Eddie Messenger, who came from Yorkshire. Will was still working at the age of 70 when Messenger told him that he had to leave the cottage they had occupied all his working life. He gave them twelve weeks to get out. Elizabeth and Will took Messenger to a tribunal and were allowed to remain for six months or until they found a suitable place to live.

Elizabeth said that she never expected they would be turned out as the family had such a long connection with the farm at Galton. They looked for a house in Owermoigne, where they would have been very happy to settle, but none was available for rent. They moved finally to a gardener's cottage outside Broadmayne a few miles away but she often came back to

Owermoigne. Elizabeth attended the open day at the church in September 2013. It was well attended and she sat in a pew most of the afternoon talking to old friends.

Norrie Woodall

Norrie's memories of the war in Owermoigne are found in the previous chapter. She lived to the great age of nearly 105 on her own in the house at the edge of the village she had occupied since before the war. She merited a full page obituary in *The Times* when she died in 2011 as the last of the Hardy Players, a drama group set up by the author during the Thirties to perform dramatisations of his stories. Thomas Hardy was already in his eighties, but the players gave him renewed interest in reworking some of his best loved stories. Norrie joined the players at 16 and spent her life talking and writing about the memories of those times. In the original troupe, Norrie's sister, Gertrude Bulger played Tess in *Tess of the D'Urbervilles* which was very popular. It is said that Florence Hardy, the poet's young second wife, was intensely jealous of her and had the players disbanded. Norrie spent the latter part of her life trying to get the players relaunched.

On Norrie's hundredth birthday, the New Hardy Players gave their first performance in Owermoigne village hall. *Under the Greenwood Tree* had a cast of twenty amateur players with local costumes and traditional Dorset accents. They subsequently performed many times throughout Dorset in church halls and large country homes and gardens. In Owermoigne they did outdoor performances at the rectory in the village and Moignes Court. Norrie contributed £1,000 from the proceeds of her memoirs to the New Hardy Players.[3] She enjoyed frequent engagements in the county including a Thomas Hardy event at the home of Julian Fellowes (author of *Downton Abbey*) and his wife (a Kitchener and Lady-in-Waiting to the Queen) in West Stafford. Her single-minded goal to relaunch the Hardy Players doubtless helped to keep her going to her great age.

---

[3] Norrie's Tale, Lulworth Cove, Lullworde Publication, 2006.

Norrie Woodhall in 'Under the Greenwood Tree'

The New Hardy Players

Chapter Four

People at the Court

Cecil and Dolly: More than half a century on the estate

During the war the military police commandeered Moignes Court. Cecil Cree and his wife, Dolly moved to East Farm House at the centre of the village on Church Lane. After the war, Dolly did not wish to leave her "dolls' house" as she called it, in fact a substantial eighteenth-century house with a large garden. Cecil had inherited the estate in 1902 on the death of his father and ran it until just before his death 59 years later.

Dolly, who became his wife, was quite a village character. She took to wearing bright waistcoats and dirndl skirts in the Swiss peasant style with coils of plats around her ears. It must have been quite popular at the time as Christopher Lloyd's mother of the celebrated garden at Great Dixter in Sussex also was pictured in his books similarly dressed. In the summers, Dolly would take her children "camping" at Holworth and had her brass bedstead moved there and had fresh milk delivered each day. It was Dolly who first suggested that her son George and Pam marry: "an arranged marriage, Dorset style," said Pam. Dolly lived to 84, cared for in her dotage by her spinster daughter, Cecily.

Captain Cecil O'Shaughnessy Cree, as he called himself, used the additional Irish surname which remains a mystery to the family. Although they are associated with the names of

Macmahon and Creagh in County Clare, O'Shaughnessy does not figure in the family lineage. Cecil struggled for years to keep the estate going, selling off land to pay mounting debts. He put the houses of the village and land up for sale in 1926. He had four or five people working on the farm and started tenanting the land he did not use. Cecil always opposed having a pub in the village. When he gave the land for the construction of the village hall, he created an adjacent reading room. This became the Cricket Club in the 1960s, the village drinking club after his death.

George and Pam: Modernising farming and management

George took over the estate in 1958 after a career in the artillery, latterly training the armies of East Africa. He had been evacuated at Dunkirk and later served in the Italian campaign. He had little introduction to farm management, having always been treated like a hired hand by his father when he was around. He married Pam in 1946 – George's mother Dolly and Pam's mother had been great friends. They enjoyed a Swiss skiing holiday together before the First World War. When Pam's family came to Dorchester from London for summer holidays, they often got together with the Cree family, thus introducing George and Pam to one another in childhood. Pam's grandfather was Alfred Pope, a solicitor, who became the owner of the Dorchester brewery which bore the family name. He shrewdly waited until the railway had come to Dorchester to buy into the enterprise, as loading stations were then developed on the rails as it passed through the precincts of the Eldridge Pope Brewery. This greatly expanded sales outside the county. The house brands

George Cree

Moignes Court

were Royal Oak and Thomas Hardy Ale, a strong beer. Hardy was a great friend of Alfred Pope. Alfred had 15 children and two lavish homes, one in town and the other at Wrackleford, just outside Dorchester.

Pam was the daughter of a wealthy businessman and his wife from the Pope family. They had met during the First World War in France where her mother was serving as a nurse, an occupation of well-born English women at the time. Pam enjoyed a privileged childhood in St John's Wood, north London. Pam and George came to make their home at Moignes Court in 1958. Until then the court had been let while George's parents remained in the village at East Farm House. They moved in with two children, Martin and Christine; their daughter Anne was born later.

George modernised and mechanised the farm, worked and managed it with a single stockman. It was a mixed farm of arables with a beef herd. He reared poultry for domestic use and quite rare Indian runner ducks from Indonesia. There was an orchard and a kitchen garden. George continued tenanting land to the Swaffield family, as his father had done. At the time, an old woman named Winnie Door lived at adjacent Hartnell Farm and used to drive her cattle up the Moreton Road, but mostly they wandered around the village untended.

George took a major interest in managing the land and drained the fields to make them more useable. He also developed an area for the conservation of a rare species of butterfly, according to the Dorset Butterfly Records Officer (January 2010). He contributed records to various local butterfly registers. In 2006, the Dorset Butterfly

Conservation Trust organised a butterfly and moth day on the estate and found 21 different species. Of particular note was the Brimstone butterfly, strikingly lime green in colour with orange spots on the wings, which is relatively rare. George provided the local record. In 1980 George decided to retire and built a cottage on the estate for himself and Pam. They celebrated their fiftieth and sixtieth wedding anniversaries there. George served on the parish council and as a school governor and churchwarden. They attended church regularly. Pam, who is 90, still enjoys attending village hall activities and is often collected by her daughters who live locally, since she no longer drives. She tries to attend as many functions as she can and is frequently at coffee mornings and the Saturday village market. With her son and daughter-in-law, she attends church as often as she can, sitting in the customary family pew near the front.

Martin and Anne: A businessman keen on hunting

Martin, George's eldest son and heir, attended Sherborne School, Balliol College, Oxford and London Business School, starting his career in marketing with Unilever. In 1977 he joined his mother's family firm, the Eldridge Pope Brewery in Dorchester. In 1982, he moved Ann, his wife and two young sons into Moignes Court. There were many changes to be made to the house including the installation of central heating. Martin had been taught estate management by George and worked on the farm when he was a student, but had no interest in taking on the farm himself. He kept on the existing tenancies and tenanted the land his father had farmed.

Martin helped develop the wine business and new brands for Eldridge Pope which was transforming the business from a traditional ale merchant. The brewery owned 200 pubs in Dorset and Hampshire. He worked for the business for nearly twenty years. The listed Victorian building in the centre of Dorchester which had been the brewery was recently renovated as a residential and leisure complex.

When he left Eldridge Pope, Martin searched throughout the county for a local business as he and the family wished to remain in Dorset. It was not easy. He finally purchased a small business in Swanage which makes wire racks for postcards and other presentational materials. He ran this business until his retirement in 2012. For fifteen years he and Anne hosted shooting parties for pheasant reared on the estate, hosting six or seven lunches a year. It was a hobby which ensured his place among the Dorset gentry.

Moignes Court also hosted deer stalking of both native roe deer and the larger sika deer. The latter were first introduced to Brownsea Island in Poole Harbour, but were sturdy enough to swim to the mainland at low tides. On the estate they eventually had to reduce the size of the deer herds to maintain the stock by ensuring that there is enough fodder for winter survival in natural locations such as Wareham Forest. Martin learned a great deal about deer stalking from the local chap who had stalking rights on the estate. The venison was butchered and frozen for family consumption. The rooms of the house are adorned with large heads and antlers. Organised shooting parties have not continued but Martin still enjoys shooting on other estates and has a great deal more time to do so since retiring. He has also had more time to consider the management of the estate and has organised further drainage.

Martin's two sisters live in local properties which belonged to the estate. Christine built a new house on the land at the back of the old schoolhouse when it was sold, moving back to the village from abroad in 2010. She retired from being an occupational therapist and worked in Dorchester hospital and before that in Lausanne hospital. Ann lives with her husband and sons in a handsomely converted building which had been a barn in Holworth. They moved to the village from London.

Martin was on the parish council for 20 years, serving for many years as chairman, as his father had done before him. He was a school governor and a member of the parochial parish council which is in charge of church affairs. Martin is the chair of the local Conservative Association and frequently hosts functions for the party. He and Anne are hospitable and often entertain local professional, business people and other land owners. They organised an open house party for the Grand National in 2013 to raise funds for the local Conservative Party. They have hosted carol concerts and held wine and cheese parties in aid of church funds. They hosted the local schoolchildren for a history afternoon at the court. Martin chaired the committee for the celebration of the Royal Wedding in 2011 seeking donations from many local businesses in order to present commemorative gifts to all the children, as had been so done in years gone by for royal occasions. The Crees have also hosted performances of the Hardy Players.

Anne was a primary schoolteacher in London prior to her

marriage. She has always been very interested in the welfare of local people, a tradition which was encouraged by her mother. She has always visited village people who are ill or too old to be active. She has for years called in on new arrivals to the village. Anne started a playgroup when her sons were young in the old Gospel Hall which she ran for the all young village children for three years. She also started a Sunday school with Jill which they ran for many years.

Ralph and Dizzi: a novel future for the estate

Ralph, Martin and Anne's eldest son, will inherit the estate. His brother, Alex is a painter who lives in London. Ralph has a degree in music and religion from the School of Oriental and African Studies, University of London, and has always been interested in the music of India and Africa. He is an accomplished drummer who teaches throughout the local school system and privately. He has a band which practises weekly in a barn behind the house. Ralph lives in a wing of Moignes Court with his wife, Dizzi (married in 2012), who is also a percussionist and plays the dulcimer, a Tudor court instrument introduced from Persia.

Ralph's drumming started in 2004 and was established with a full diary after three years. His company is called Magic Drum and there is a Magic Drum Orchestra of fifteen musicians who play at music festivals throughout the country. With a colleague, Ralph does African drumming workshops for corporate clients, people with special needs, children and retired people. Having spent a great deal on their website and online promotion, the business has now begun to flourish.

Drumming is Ralph's great passion. He enjoys working with young people. The schools programme is linked to the Dorset Area Schools Partnership which promotes music teaching. He also plays the piano and guitar. Ralph composes on software using a wide variety of musical instruments in the tradition of world music. He likes to reserve two days a week for composing and recording and would like to have the time to do more. Ralph meditates one hour a day and complements this with physical exercise. He has a keen interest in religious philosophy.

Dizzi established a company for importing or commissioning dulcimers (from the three craftsmen who make them in the UK) which she sells online. She first started as a drummer, but found that she always had a tune in her head. She first heard the dulcimer played by a busker and fell in love with the instrument. She and Ralph have been busking during the summer holidays. Dizzi comes from Somerset. Having left home at 16, she travelled and camped with anti-road protesters and learned to play the drums in the evenings round a campfire. At 19 she moved to London to try to get work with different bands. She did a City and Guilds course in music production and technology and bought her first dulcimer in 2000. She has a degree in music production from the University of Bath and prints and distributes music for the dulcimer on the website. She has set up a recording company and hopes to do more recording with Ralph. They call themselves, "The Crees" when they perform together.

Ralph and Dizzi have an organic garden producing all their own vegetables and fruit. Ralph cannot ever imagine himself as a farmer. They would like to develop the estate initially into a refuge for busy urban people who would like to spend quality time in a rural environment. They envisage housing clients in comfortable tents in the woodland on the estate. Clients could have their meals brought to them, allowing them as much isolation and solitude as they wished.

Ralph and Dizzi envisage the future of the estate as a community. They cannot see themselves living alone in the large house with their children (first born, December 2013). People could live in yurts, large family size Mongolian-style tents of which they already have one. While they plan to retain ownership of the land and the farm tenancies, people would be given an opportunity to live and work on the farm communally, but living separately. As some members of the community might well have jobs elsewhere, they envisage that they could exchange work or payment for gardening, maintenance and food preparation with others. They plan to share the historic large court room for meetings and workshops.

Ralph and Dizzi feel that the estate is too large and too beautiful for them to live and work on their own, although they plan to retain final say on management decisions. They are very keen on communal activities and promoting group activities, while retaining personal family ties. They envisage that people could commit themselves to several communal activities and responsibilities. They would consider starting a local free school on the estate in which the community members might take turns teaching. Childcare could also be a communal crèche or nursery, also managed communally.

In the coming years Ralph and Dizzi plan to visit other

experiments like the one they would like to create to see how they work. There is time as the plan is for decades ahead: at the moment, it has the status of a dream with rather vague ideas which they are gathering as they go along. They have discussed their ideas with Anne and Martin, who enjoy a very different lifestyle, but are very supportive. Ralph discusses some current ideas on estate management with his father, but he feels that he can wait until the time comes when the keys will be handed over and they will be in a position to make their own decisions. Martin is only 66 and still very active, so their plans will only take shape in a decade or two.

Chapter Five

Farmers, Plantsmen, Caravans: The Village Economy

Employment in farming is in steady decline all over England. Owermoigne and the surrounding area still have a substantial number of working farms, but they employ few people and rely on contractors. Large numbers of farmers have been driven out by the steep rise in costs particularly animal feeds, disease problems in the herds and persistent volatile weather over the past decade. Farm incomes have fallen sharply, especially due to tight margins negotiated by the large supermarket chains. Dairy farming much publicised in 2012-13 with a fall of 43 per cent. Without alternative skills and training, many farmers have felt trapped in a downward spiral and calls for help to dedicated helplines such as the Royal Agricultural Benevolent Institution have increased dramatically in consequence. Suicide among farmers became a serious issue, particularly well known to the rector in Owermoigne who serves on the Salisbury Diocese Farming and Rural Affairs Commission. In the last fifteen years the number of dairy farmers has been reduced by half. Those who remain have had to make major changes in the way they farm.

An article by a local farmer in the parish magazine (January and August 2013) pointed out that the wet weather of the summer of 2012 and the cold winter had been hot topics of local conversation. The grain harvest was down by one third; consequently there was less forage in winter for the cows, requiring the purchase of additional feed at high prices. As world grain supplies were very tight, prices rose in an unrelenting spiral. The wet, cold summer of 2012 slowed everything down. The delay in harvesting, reduced sowing and cold spring conditions meant that the 2013 harvest, while in drier conditions, was significantly down on average.[1]

Dorset farmers had never known the water table to be so high. They had to plant spring cereals which typically yield less than their winter equivalents. The exceedingly warm weather in the summer of 2013 created significant new problems. And then there was the never ending rain of early 2013 when the low-lying fields were flooded and the water table was exceedingly high, with mud everywhere making winter work very difficult. As the Met Office predicts more volatility in the weather to come in longer cycles, there is a great deal of concern throughout the farming communities.

Milk yields improved for dairy farmers, but it had been an exceptionally expensive winter requiring the purchase of additional feed. The financial legacy of the past few years will be felt by farmers for the coming two to three years. They have begun to use new techniques for increasing maize crop yields like covering them with strips of biodegradable plastic to get them to germinate more quickly. Margins are still very tight for dairy farmers. Milk supplies were reduced by 8.4 per cent which caused buyers to chase supply and forced prices upwards again, which was very welcome![2]

---

[1] Defra, National Statistics, Farm Business Income, 2012-13, 31 October, 2013.
[2] Nick Cobb, Northground Dairy, West Chaldon, Dorset, *Compass*, January 2013, p. 19; August 2013, p. 23.

Glebe Farm: Seasonal Turkeys

John was on his tractor when I arrived. He was shifting old Leyland cypress trees which had been removed behind his house. He showed me the espalier fruit trees in the orchard which would replace these and cover the breeze block wall of the main barn. He is now 81 years old and a long-time member of the parish council. His son, Mark, who lives next door, runs the farm. John was delighted to tell me that they had a male heir who is very young. When he was born, it prompted John's wife Anne to look into the family history.

Local farms are typically a family affair passed on from one generation to another. John's great-grandfather farmed at Tyneham and Kimmerage. His father began as a tenant at the village of Corfe Castle, then at Broadmayne and East Knighton with mixed farming of dairy, beef, sheep, pigs and poultry. They made their own butter and cheese. John went to agricultural college at Kingston Maurward and was exempted from military service because he was farming with his father, for whom he worked until 1950. He was active in a discussion club for farmers during the war, where they exchanged ideas on efficient food production.

John met his wife Anne when she was dancing in a variety show in Weymouth. She came from Liverpool and while they were courting, John went to London to see her in several of her shows. Initially they lived in a cottage on the family farm. Their first farm in 1965 was fifty acres of arables at Warmwell. John then took over the management of the farm at Watercombe, which belonged to his cousin. They purchased 33 acres opposite the village on the Wareham

Road and a bungalow. Having added land from time to time, the farm is now 220 acres.

In 1990 they started a Christmas turkey business, beginning with fifty chicks. Today they rear 1,000. The business is well-known throughout the county, and in the days leading up to the holiday season there is a large car park and long queues. The birds are purchased from a breeder in Essex in June and they are reared on the farm. The turkeys do not require much land – only five acres. John and Mark built several new buildings for the business and are at full capacity presently and would have to build further to expand. They would finance expansion from their own resources, not a grant, customarily reserved for bigger projects. Initially there were five other local farm suppliers of seasonal turkeys, but most of them dropped out because of increasingly exacting health and safety requirements, which add considerably to the expense of production.

The turkeys are plucked each year by twenty hired hands and hung for twelve days prior to Christmas sales. Polish people have been hired year on year and are regarded as excellent workers. A few years ago they hired local people, but found them less than satisfactory. The turkey farming works well together with arable production, as the turkeys graze during the summer and require little work when the harvesting has to be done. Once the harvest is in, they start working on the turkeys in November and December. They considered doing a "Pick Your Own" fruit and vegetable farm as they have an excellent location on the main road, but thought better of it as it would have been difficult to fit into the annual timetable. With the revenue from the business they were able to purchase additional land in 1996 to raise beef cattle, but the herd were affected by BSE and foot and mouth disease and had to be reduced from 200 to 30. They lost money on it. They now have 300 acres in arables: rape, barley and wheat plus peas and oats for turkey feed. They expect the price of these to continue to rise because of world shortages and growing demand.

John and Anne have always been very active in the local Conservative Party and farming organisations including the National Farmers Union and the Dorset Agricultural Society. They support the Dorset Young Farmers. When Mark was married and started his family, they moved into the original bungalow. John and Anne built themselves a fine house of Purbeck stone and brick on an adjacent plot with some hired professionals and craftsmen, spending only £15,000 on materials and labour.

Mark was born on his grandfather's farm and has lived at the present location since he was 14. He married Jo in 2001 and was proud to say that her grandfather was a farmer in Buckinghamshire. He feels that they have a more diverse group of friends than his parents, not just in the farming community. I asked him about his young son and daughter. What if his son did not wish to inherit the farm? He and Jo said that would be OK. And if their daughter were more interested, that would be OK, too. But clearly for farmers, sons are customarily regarded as crucial to the future of the business.

Holly Farm: A Holstein Herd

Alfie had not had a holiday for 26 years until his son, Max, took over the farm when he retired. For the past ten years, Alfie and his wife, Frieda, have spent the winters at La Gomera in the Canary Islands where they bought a small house in a beautiful ravine. Alfie goes fishing and they walk and drive around the island and enjoy eating out. Frieda is also from a farming family from North Dorset: "You have to be born into this life," she said. Alfie's father bought Holly Farm in 1955 when he was demobbed from the army. It had been unoccupied for a long time and much work was needed to make it productive. Alfie developed a skill in repairing farm equipment. He still loves doing it and his activities until now have been important for keeping costs low. He is never happier than when stripping down a long-serving piece of equipment to try to put it back into service.

Max and his wife, Amy, who also comes from a local farming family, live in a recently constructed timber bungalow on the farm behind his parents' home. They lived formerly at Watercombe Farm where Max farmed 400 tenanted acres until the estate was put up for auction. Max would have loved to have purchased the farm, but it proved to be beyond his means. He has been working with his father since he was eight when he learned to drive a tractor. Max and Amy moved to the village in 2010. Amy did the paperwork for the farm, including passports for each of the cows with their medical and productive history. Until recently she also did the financials, but with the anticipated expansion, they now have an accountant.

They had a bovine TB scare ten years ago and Defra ordered fifty cows to be culled for examination. They proved to be clean, but it cost them dear – a loss of £100,000. Max sent a letter to the local Labour MP, Jim Knight, and got a form reply. Richard Drax, who was then getting ready to contest the seat for the Conservatives in 2005, heard about the problem from the local NFU. and drove to the farm to talk to them. He took notes and said that he would do what he could. Drax had an excellent reputation with local farmers and was elected.

Max has now taken over the farm and is on a journey he described as "very exciting" to introduce robotic management of the herd and increase it to 650. It will come on stream in late 2014. He spent some years researching the potential future of the farm, and given the tight margins for dairy farming, he decided on the installation of robotic feeding and milking. This enables the cows to be fed and milked on demand. Each animal will have a bracelet with a transponder to identify it on the system. The system monitors the milk levels and can detect problems very quickly which are then dispatched by message to the mobile phone of the herdsman in charge. There will be four double robot stations in the large new barn complex. Each cow has its own "bed". They will remain in the barn complex except for three months of the year when they will be out in the field "on maternity leave". They will return to a special transition barn which serves as a "maternity ward".

Holly Farm comprises 850 acres, part tenanted, part owned, in grass and mixed feed, including maize for the herd. The seeding and harvesting is done by a local contractor. They have six employees in the dairy, having expanded to anticipate the new fully automated venture. Currently they produce 4.6 million litres of milk per year exclusively for Marks & Spencer, which is also used for butter and ice cream. It is very high quality milk with low saturated fat.

The herd are all Holsteins, which were described as high input and high output: each produces 11,000lts of milk a year and will produce for about seven to eight years. Holsteins are somewhat delicate, not hardy, and require considerable care.

Max selected the robotic equipment from Holland, the most advanced system he could source (developed in the last ten years). It is strong and robust, predicted to last 25-30 years. The firm will install the equipment and train the herdsmen, half of whom are Romanian. Max said that he has tried to work with local people, but found that the immigrant workers were much more effective, without "issues" and willing to work very hard including night work, a common story of farm labour in the area. The new system will work on a twenty-four-hour cycle.

Robotics had already been introduced to dairy farming in Britain and Ireland, but Holly Farm will now be one of the largest installations in the UK and will possibly expand further, if the business plan and estimates work out. The project costing several million pounds is financed by bank loans. Max acquired a consultant who was introduced to him by Marks & Spencer, and was essential to securing the loan. The consultant developed the business plan and will continue to monitor the project for four to five years.

Amy's mother, Sandra, also lives in the village. She is from a farming family which farmed 5,000 acres at one time farther to the southwest near Portesham. Sandra's brother, Paul (now retired) was a tenant on the Moignes Court estate, a tenancy he inherited from his father. At his principal farm Paul set up the Great Dorset Maize Maze several years ago which attracted up to 25,000 visitors a year. To start out he contacted a well-known maze designer who made the design with a satellite photo and then marked out the field before the maize was planted. The farm buildings were used for family entertainments.

Sandra is a counsellor working for Dorset County Council with children of 8-13 who experience difficulties at school or at home. She has been very active raising funds for children's activities in the village including the playground. She has also organised activities on forest life and wildlife, although very few children came to these events. Sandra greatly enjoys looking after her grandchildren, six of whom are the children of Dorset farmers. She has left her job and has set up a small online business of knitted garments. Her latest creations are knitted wigs which are very popular, as a novel costume for performers or for women who have lost their hair through cancer treatment. They are sold on American craft websites as patterns. She would like to build the business further while retaining the design role. Sandra recently decided to start up a dance evening in the village hall which she is hoping will be popular.

Watercombe Farm: A New Enterprise

Alison and Andrew bought the farm of 200 acres with a house and numerous outbuildings in 2010. They came from Wiltshire where they owned a farm of comparable size which they worked for eighteen years. They looked for properties all over the South West for two years, using several decisive criteria in order to make their choice: good access, few restrictions and the possibility for diversification. They ranked each of these as they viewed different farms. The condition of the house that came with the property was a low priority: they had already renovated two houses and knew they could do it again. They felt that Watercombe had great potential, and were keen on the location near the coast.

Farms of this size – 200 acres – make it difficult to turn a profit, Andrew said. The main problem becomes insufficient capital to renew the machinery. But his previous experience has been a great help: he had been in a business with his father buying, renewing and reselling farm machinery and therefore is able to do much of the maintenance himself. They grow arables throughout the year including rape in August, and winter barley in September-October (later in 2012 because of the wet summer). The land is not suitable for double cropping.

Andrew's grandfather had been a farmer in Somerset. Alison's father was a farmer whom she described as very committed and a workaholic, which almost persuaded her never to marry a farmer. But the decision to go into farming was a joint one after they were married. They have two sons at the start of their careers working in financial services.

There is a beautiful bridleway that goes alongside the farm following the chalk ridge from Holworth. Watercombe is a very old farm with ancient homesteads apparently located nearby. After some recent storms when the rain washed the pebbles into the farm, they found a flint arrowhead. When Andrew cleared a barn with the cattle pens, they realised they could stable horses. They restored the old dairy building to a high standard and have developed a DIY livery for horses which now has twenty horses, nine of which can be stabled. They have to maintain the electric fences and check during lightning storms or local fireworks whether the horses have bolted, as they do not always feel the shock through their thick winter blankets. Andrew and Alison have built a tack and tearoom for the owners. The horses require quite a lot of work in season to keep the pastures mowed and tidy. It is great horse country along the chalk ridge of the downs and beyond.

Andrew and Alison have rebuilt the old barn which had beautiful old stonework and have obtained planning permission to turn it into their new home. They plan to do most of the work themselves, except for the electrical work and plumbing. They have no employees on the farm: Andrew's father helps with the harvest. In the winter they work on the buildings and equipment. They both remain very optimistic about their work and the future of the farm. Both have a strong positive attitude and have said that sometimes farmers are too pessimistic and gloomy. It is not easy work year on year but they seem to love it.

Alison has started a sideline, a business renting party furniture, which they had purchased secondhand for the celebration of their twenty-fifth wedding anniversary in 2012. They held the event in the grain store which was empty in the summer: it was covered in white bunting and seated 130 people for the occasion. In the first summer Alison rented the furniture about six times. But there are already bookings (early 2014) for the summer, including a wedding to be held in a marquee on the farm.

Alison is a committed Christian, who took a great deal of time after they relocated to the area to find a congregation she wished to join. She finally settled into the Ebenezer Church in Dorchester after attending services at eight others. She misses the church in Wiltshire where she and her family worshipped and where her brother is a lay preacher. Andrew does not follow her path and their sons have their own minds about their religious commitment, she said.

Holworth Farm: Dairy Farming on the Ridge

John and his wife, Kim, came from Yarlington in Somerset where they had a dairy farm. They were bought out, and they purchased Holworth Farm in 1992. It is 200 acres with a herd of 200. They are an organic farm which is very "hands on" as it is not big enough to hire employees. They "went organic" in 2001 and the first year the grass turned yellow; it was like coming off drugs not using fertiliser for the first time. It was better the second year, and by the third year they had wonderful red and white clover which is very nutritious for the herd, together with wonderful wildlife. They use homeopathic remedies for the herd, purchased from a farm in Yorkshire. If an animal is ill, they send them milk and hair from an affected cow and the firm send them a concentrated drink based on the animal's profile. Organic feed is very expensive.

Charlie, their son, is 19 and has a diploma in agriculture from Kingston Maurward. He is interested in taking over the farm: "We tried to discourage him, but we did not succeed," John said. Farming is tough and if Charlie had not been so keen, we would have sold by now. With the recession, the price of organic milk has dropped to nearly non-organic levels, which makes the margins very small. Their daughter is a journalist and works in London.

Pig Farming in Holworth

Richard has a small pig farm on his father's land. His mother is from a local family and inherited 75 acres of land. His father's family had a chicken farm in Ansty, and moved to the land in Holworth to pasture organic beef and sheep. Richard went to Thornlow, the boys' private school in Weymouth, also attended by Max of Holly Farm. With a diploma from Kingston Maurward, he does a variety of farm jobs locally. He also sells and installs fencing for gardens, stock and farming. He lived in a caravan on his parents' farm until he purchased a bungalow in the village.

Galton Farm

Edwin, the owner of this local farm, adjacent to the village on the east side, is also Master of the South Down Hunt. He came from Cumbria to Dorset in order to purchase a larger farm. There are 670 acres which he owns jointly with a business partner who lives in a cottage on the estate. The farm was pretty run- down when they bought it. Initially they tried dairy, but only rear beef cattle now. The supermarket prices for milk were so ruthless that they decided to get out of dairy farming. They use contractors for seeding and harvesting. The large house on the estate was built about 1860 from bricks made in a brickworks on the farm. There are three farm cottages on the estate which used to be for employees but are now rented or have been sold.

Galton is in the Domesday Book: it was named in Old English – *gagol* means bog myrtle or sweet gale plus the word *tun* for settlement or subject to *gafol* or tax. The Galton family, including several prominent industrialists and scientists, can be traced to the hamlet in the seventeenth century. The family has been described as being exceptionally intelligent. They were Quakers who moved to the industrial towns of the midlands and the North. John Galton was a member of the Royal Society in the eighteenth century, a successful entrepreneur who also wrote about birds, canals and scientific instruments. He had a gun manufacturing business which got him into trouble with his Quaker congregation, but he put up a spirited defence and remained.

The most celebrated Galton family member was Francis Galton (1822-1911), a polymath half cousin of Charles Darwin, who invented the weather map and statistical concepts such as standard deviation and regression. The Galton Laboratory at University College, London, is named after him. He was also an anthropologist, explorer, eugenicist, geographer and inventor, publishing prodigiously in his lifetime. Galton developed differential whistle tests to examine hearing ability, devised questionnaires for researching human settlements, and invented a method for classifying fingerprints. But he is best known as the main British spokesman for the pseudo-science of eugenics, which was quite popular before the First World War. It fuelled arguments of racial superiority.

Misery Farm

A paved track runs nearly a mile from the road past a large lake until one arrives at the farm. The origin of the rather strange name is not known. Some surmise that it had been a clandestine pleasure ground for the Warmwell estate several miles south. The seventeenth-century maps show the farm as Misery Farm when Warmwell House was built. Don, who spent his childhood on the Dorset coast near Tyneham, bought the farm in 1983 in a very dilapidated state. There is a beef herd of 150 and some prize hens. Now it has two good farmhouses, both of which are used for holiday lettings.

Farming in Wool; Living in the Village

Until his retirement, Mike managed a beef herd and raised prize South Down bulls, the largest domestic breed, on a farm just outside Wool. He and his wife, Pam, have lived in their present bungalow in the village since 1973 having bought the house off the initial plans. They were farming at Bradford Peverel, west of Dorchester at the time when the farm was sold and they looked for a new home.

Mike was born in Wool, but not into a farming family. His father was the foreman of a railway gang maintaining the tracks. He became interested in farming from a young age when he joined the Young Farmers Union which was then very active and organised competitions among local chapters. Mike had been mole trapping since the age of eight and he sent the pelts to Cambridge earning 10p. He later branched into fox and badger pelts which remained a small side-earner once he started farming. The most he was ever paid for the fox pelt was £27 in the 1970s. In his retirement, Mike was described to me as "the red hot mole man" by a neighbour when I was searching for services. Mike was kept busy by many people in the village. He cycled around to clients and asked that a donation was left in an envelope at the church marked "moles" when his services were finished.

They met in 1954 when Pam was working as a dairymaid at Woolbridge Manor, on the River Frome on the edge of Wool, celebrated as the location of Tess and Angel's wedding night in Hardy's *Tess of the D'Urbervilles*. Pam was staying locally with her grandmother: she came originally from Worchester. Mike had worked at Woolbridge prior to serving in the army in Korea. There was such a local shortage of labour that Mike was offered four farm management jobs when he was demobbed, but he decided to try another career initially. They married in 1957 and he joined the Prison Service as a discipline officer, first serving in Oxford where Pam worked, initially on the buses and later doing car upholstery at the Morris plant. When the service became aware of Mike's interest in farming they posted him first to a borstal farm in Yorkshire, and later to a prison farm in Tadnoll which is on the heath land between Owermoigne and Wool.

The contract for the Bradford Peverel dairy farm lasted for six years where they both worked with a herd of 70, and cared for all the calves from four farms of the owner. Pam said she earned £1 a day and during all that time they never had a day off. They managed to save up for their own house, though. In the same year that they moved to Owermoigne, Mike launched a new farm for a civil engineer just outside Wool. It was all beef with 200 animals, including the prize South Devons, which were shown all over the South West and at London shows. It became a very valuable pedigree herd for its owner.

Pam worked at the officer's mess at Bovington during this period serving daily and working at special officers' dinners. They had children at the time who attended middle school in

Puddletown. The children used to cycle to Crossways to catch the bus, as none came as far as the village. If Pam was doing an early or late shift on the base, Mike was at home for the children. It was quite a hard life in those years. After that Pam tended the patisserie counter in Waitrose in Dorchester for ten years. She is a fantastic baker and sells goods at the village market each month. Both Mike and Pam keep fit going to the gym five days a week in Wareham. Mike cycles all around the area and they look after their young grandchildren after school on Thursdays and all day on Saturday. Their son, Graham, has a clay-pigeon shooting business near Wool, and his wife is a hairdresser. Another granddaughter has just been recruited to the Metropolitan Police.

Mill House Nurseries

Old maps of the area indicate the mill, which was first identified in the Domesday Book. Derek and his family bought the Mill House and surrounding land in 1962 after he returned from military service in Nigeria and had worked for the Ministry of Agriculture for several years. He and his family were looking to buy a business in the countryside. The family included his brother, who continued to work in London, and his retired parents. The property was advertised as a mill, trout stream and seven acres. It had already been developed as a plant nursery.

The extended family have always been collectors, starting with glass and antique clocks. They eventually created a small interesting museum on the property with these collections, including a rather wonderful four-poster Chinese bed, which once belonged to an uncle. The next venture was to acquire a cider press, as there was an apple orchard on the property which produced a large crop every year. Derek initially used an old press, and added several derelict ones he found in Dorset and surrounding counties to his collection. This eventually became a cider museum to complement the glass and clocks. The aim of the Mill House cider-making was to get back to the rich traditional cider of the eighteenth and nineteenth centuries. In the first year they produced 300 gallons and obtained an off licence for direct sales. They increased the production to 3,500 gallons within a few years.

The nursery was developed into an extensive horticulture business, very much a family affair of Derek, his wife Mary, whom he married in 1977, and their daughters. Mary was born in the village and had initially trained as a dental hygienist prior to joining the family business full time. It is a year-round business, beginning with seeds and seed potatoes which arrive in winter. For the rest of the year they specialise in superior house and garden plants including an extensive collection of pelargonium, hanging baskets and a wide variety of vegetable and herb seedlings. They have two large greenhouses and various polytunnels and are renowned for the large variety and quality of their plants. They have a regular customer base.

Derek was a founding member of the village cricket team, was on the parish council, chaired the village hall committee, and sang in the church choir. But once the horticulture business developed, he had little time for these. An abiding memory is of Derek and his brother swapping clues for *The Times* crossword with the nursery full of weekend customers.

Mills Nursery

Jimmy came to the village from Cockfosters in North London which he described as a lovely place to live, apart from the anti-aircraft noise during the war. He had been evacuated to Cambridgeshire together with seventeen other local children and they had a whale of a time with haywains and horse-drawn wagons. As local labour was scarce, the children helped get the harvest in.

After the war, Jimmy and his mother were on holiday in Weymouth and cycled to Owermoigne. They saw a house they liked and asked the owners if they would be interested in selling. It was very basic with a privy and running water only in the outside shed. But they bought it in 1947 and moved from London. Mother bought a Guernsey cow which was the beginning of a small dairy business. They also raised pigs and poultry (7-800 chickens). For 15 years Jimmy did an egg round to regular customers in Weymouth.

Jimmy's mother was a pacifist and very outspoken about it. In court, a judge once told her that she was the most aggressive pacifist he ever met. She was quite a local character, well remembered in the village and served as a church warden. When she was 70 she found herself in court again, this time on a drink driving charge.

In 1960 they began to sell bedding plants for the shops and set up a retail nursery. There were so many successful local nurseries that they finally closed the retail business in 2005. For thirty years they have had a stall at the Sunday market in Dorchester and also added Yeovil and Bridport markets. But the local councils privatised the markets and the stallholder fees went up dramatically, so they had to cut back. Jimmy continues to sell plants at the Dorchester market to the local post office/shops. He rents out a few caravan sites on a field next to the nursery.

Benville Nurseries

Jill S. was resident in the village from 1952 when she and her husband were married in the village church. She had lived with her parents in Crossways where they had the local post office after the war, which she described as nothing more than a wooden shack. Crossways was a very small village at the time. Her first memory of Owermoigne was cycling to piano lessons on the Wareham Road. Jill and her husband founded the Benville Nursery. Shel was the church secretary for 25 years and said that she remembered many of the people buried in the churchyard. She was president of the local WI and was widely known and loved in the village. She died in 2011.

The nursery was taken over by Jill's niece, Jill W., who had a degree in horticulture from Kingston Maurward and worked as a landscape gardener. The bungalow was affordable because it had an agricultural tie, which ensured that the purchase price was affordable. The business is just about ticking over and includes shrubs, vegetable plants and hanging baskets. The holding is 33 acres of field and woodland. Jill rents out livery stables to a few people and pastures horses, all of which is owner-managed, and she rents out spaces for a few caravans in the summer. She sells vegetables and plants at the monthly village market and has a stall at the end of her drive on the Moreton Road with an honesty box (which has often been robbed during the summer). She feels that she cannot expand because she cannot afford to employ anyone. She manages on her own with occasional part-time staff.

Sandyholme Caravan Park

Mike worked at the Red Lion pub in Winfrith with his father for several years prior to taking it over in 1976. Mike is Edna's son, who featured in the chapter "Wartime Memories". The pub business was substantial – doing 60-70 lunches a day in the summer months. They had three to four people in the kitchen; two behind the bar in two shifts and fifteen to twenty part-time employees, including cleaners for the B&B accommodation above the pub. The tenancy was on a three to four-year lease, but when there were major changes in the brewery industry in the 1980s, the rent increased dramatically and they decided to leave.

Mike looked around for a new enterprise as he wished to remain in Dorset. He learned that the people who owned Sandyholme on the edge of the village were thinking of selling. He was always interested in this type of business – out of doors, with the winter months off for other personal activities. And it was a "people business" to which he was accustomed. They ran the pub and the park together for the final three years of the tenancy. Then he moved his parents to Owermoigne and liquidated the debt they had.

To begin with there were 35 holiday caravans, but there was room for 60 pitches, so they expanded the business. Twenty-five of the caravans belonged to the business and thirty-five sites were rented by people who brought them in. They have camper vans and tent pitches, too. Every summer they are fully booked, with a lot of repeat business. The season runs from Easter to October. There is a shop and a bar and an extensive workshop for repairs. Mike says that it is very hard work with long hours during the season, though he has a few holiday employees, mainly young people from the village. Mike enjoys many hobbies including racing motorbikes, cycling, deep sea diving and, more recently, golf. He dives locally, fishing for lobster and scallops. He has also explored the local wrecks off the coast, and been on several expeditions abroad with the Scientific Exploration Society.

Nether Moynton: Building an Estate on Watercress and Lettuce

Peter lives on the edge of the village in a mansion in traditional style which was built to his specification in 2008 with turrets, many reception rooms, a library, conservatory and extensive gardens. Long horn sheep and Charolais cattle graze in the middle distance to enhance the view of this recent gentleman farmer. Peter was born in West Stafford, the son of the local blacksmith. As a teenager he became very interested in cars, their maintenance and repair. He learned to be a welder and worked for a car finance company. Following that experience, he bought his first garage in Puddletown and several other garages over a period of forty years. It became the largest car dealership in Dorset.

Peter's wife is from Dorchester: they met at the local tennis club. Their first home was in West Stafford, before buying a large family home in Dorchester, which today serves as the business headquarters. They have five children and ten grandchildren. In 1985 Peter bought a farm on the Moreton

Road about a mile outside the village, where he had been breeding prize bulls for more than ten years. The farm was called Nether Moynton, a name which he subsequently used for the house and the estate.

In 1994 with a keen interest in agriculture, Peter acquired several local watercress farms, a typical wetland crop of Dorset. The older native varieties used to be harvested all year round, even through the ice layers which formed in the winter, although the modern varieties are more seasonal. He called the new business the Watercress Company. He now has 500 acres and growing, planted with different varieties of lettuce and salad leaves for major supermarkets. The company developed mechanised cutting machines for harvesting the crop, helping the operation maintain very low labour costs. Initially they washed and prepared the leaves and packed them into bags for delivery.

The firm soon established itself in international agribusiness providing supermarkets with year round supplies of fresh lettuce and greens. The original business model was developed locally, but is also used in his operations in Spain and Florida where the company has 500 acres under cultivation in each. The Watercress Company became a major player in this market. Growing abroad for Tesco, ASDA, Waitrose and other major supermarkets ensured year round supply. In the UK, the crop is vulnerable to heavy rain and hailstorms.

Eventually Peter sold the packaging and distribution operations to Geest, the Dutch agribusiness firm, and concentrated on the growing. The business has a turnover of

£12 million per year. Peter also has another local business: the franchise of Massey Ferguson farm machinery.

There are countless historical examples of industrialists or businessmen buying or building a country mansion with an estate for prestige and status, which traditionally become a drain on their resources. Peter has turned this model on its head and lives surrounded by fields of fresh salad leaves, what one might call "green gold". He remains a thoroughly Dorset person, committed to local enterprise and charity. He is immensely proud of his garden and began planting trees on the estate fifteen years before building the house.

Chapter Six
The Church
History

Founded in 1333 St Michael's Church is in the centre of the village. The first rector, Edward Chaundos, was appointed in the reign of Edward III. In the Church of England, rectors were parish priests where glebe lands were available in the parish. They thus received a larger tithe than a vicar, but the allocation of the land came with the responsibility of maintaining the chancel of the church, while the parish was responsible for the repair of the rest of the building. Only the church tower remains from this early period. The remainder was rebuilt in 1883 after a fire "left it in a dilapidated and dangerous condition with the walls and roof on the point of collapse", according to the *Dorchester County Chronicle* at the time. The bells carry the date 1594 in the reign of Elizabeth I. The font is of Portland stone. There is a plaque to the Adam Jones Charity, 1653, which confirmed that he left his estate in trust for the poor of the village. The trust financed the building of Charity Cottages in 1882.

The church registers were said to be among the best kept in the Diocese of Salisbury and recorded many Hardys between 1625 and 1800. They were on display in the chancel on the occasion of the retirement of the rector in September, 2013. The church records for 1785 included the following moduses (tithes): "2d. for every milch cow, 1/- for every calf. The rector had the right to as many turves (tied bundles of heather used for fuel) from Galton Heath and other local lands as could be cut in one day with three spades on an annual basis, etc."[1] Traditionally the landed gentry were consulted on the appointment of rectors as they are still. The Cree family were active in the appointment of Richard Gregory in 1982 and the consultation process for the appointment of a new rector in 2014 includes various local land owning families. Old traditions die hard in the rural church.

A Jubilee arch over the entrance to the church grounds was dedicated in 1897 for Queen Victoria's 60th jubilee. Last year, a flagpole put in place by volunteer labour became the Jubilee emblem for Elizabeth II. The organ was installed in 1937 and played for many years by Kate McCloud, a strong village personality, who was widowed during the First World War and raised her many children on her own. It was reported that she could swear with the best of them and was often adamant and vocal about keeping children quiet in church. She was generous with the land she owned on the edge of the village and gave plots to people like the farm manager on the estate when he retired, in order to build a bungalow. Similarly, when the much admired rector, William Gallagher (in service 1945-1955) died, Mrs McCloud gave a parcel of land to his widow and daughter to build a timber bungalow (which is today my home).

The brass memorial plaque for the 1914-18 war has the names of three men from the Westmacott family who lost their lives. Adrian Victor Cree is also remembered in a plaque. He was a younger son of the family: he had gone to

---

[1] Owermoigne WI, History, Op.Cit. Ch. "The Church," n.p.

India as a tea planter, joined the Royal Welch Fusiliers and died at Ypres in 1916. The east window is dedicated to the Cree family and the west window to John Robert Cree, the rector whose legacy financed the reconstruction of the church in 1887.

The fine old rectory was home of the rectors and their families until 1977 when the village was amalgamated with the Benefice of Watercombe which includes five churches. A modern rectory was built in Broadmayne. Among the recent rectors, Richard Gregory was a keen yachtsman who spent much of his ministry building a boat in the barn next to the church, and often seemed too busy, it was said, to attend the meetings of the parochial parish council. He supported the ordination of women, but felt that the people of the village were too conservative to accept such a change. Women were already serving as curates and church wardens.

The parish magazine was founded in 1945 and began to record the non-church activities of the local villages from the late 1970s. In the early editions, the five churches of the benefice were pictured on the cover with a letter from the rector. The articles contained news about individual people, including holiday stories and recorded births, marriages and moves in and out of the locality. There was a women's page and a children's page and news about the mother's union, the WI, the mothers and babies clubs, hospital volunteers, the horticultural clubs, youth and social clubs and bingo. There were recipes for marmalade, bread and seasonal turkey stuffing. The current parish magazine of the benefice, *Compass*, remains a vital information source of all local activities.

Current Activities

It costs about £50 per day to keep the church open, most of which goes on heating costs and repairs. Many of the major renovations like the fourteenth-century tower and the repair of the roof in recent years have been financed by charities associated with the diocese. The church is open daily until dusk, tended by the church wardens. All the silver is locked away, with replicas in wood, of little value, left on display. The sacristan, a church warden, prepares the church for services and the wine and wafers for communion. The altar cloth was made by the children of Owermoigne School in 2006 before the school closed. It is handprinted, with coloured cut-outs of their hands forming a rainbow. Annual fund raising events include flower shows, a harvest festival with lunch and the annual gift day.

Only a handful of people attend services on a regular basis. The average attendance is thirteen, a number which is inflated by popular services such as Mothering Sunday, the pet service, Christmas and Easter services. The church electoral roll includes 94 people (up 20 since 2008 after a local campaign); 64 of those are in Owermoigne and 30 in the small Holworth community. Sunday services are shared among the churches of the benefice. St Catherine's, Holworth has monthly services taken by the ReverendAnthony Bush who lives in Holworth. They are well attended, as there is great local loyalty to the fine little wooden church overlooking the sea.

The parochial parish council in Owermoigne meets four times

Postcard Views of the Church

The Annual Pet Service

a year and includes the church wardens, both of whom are women, and three other elected members, a dwindling number. The annual income of the parish in 2012 was £15,600 and the expenditure just over £14,000 with £6,000 in reserve.[1] Receipts for the "gift day" of 2012 were a record, which was particularly helpful for the reserve fund, following a large increase in annual insurance costs. A fund was raised for providing new pew cushions. The parish is required to make a contribution to the Diocese of Salisbury every year, nearly £9,000 in 2012. As it is a considerable charge for such a small parish with only local fundraising capability, I asked Geoff, the treasurer, how they managed to be sure of having sufficient funds to make the charge each year. He replied with a smile, "It was God's work."

The annual pet service is very popular with the participation of ponies, dogs, guinea pigs, hamsters and rabbits. The pastor officiating customarily reads from St Francis of Assisi, "who reminded us that animals are forgiving and dependable and do not hold grudges".[2] The Christmas carol service attracts a large crowd, usually about 130 people. At this annual event, people from the village and children do the readings.

The flower festival of 2009 took place on a brilliant sunny summer evening. There were songs of praise to accompany the flower arrangements on the theme "Somewhere over the Rainbow", which adorned the church. The pew posts were

---

[1] St Michael's Church, Owermoigne, "Annual Report and Financial Statement for the Year ending 31 December 2012", February, 2013.
[2] The pet service, St Michael's Church, Owermoigne, 2009.

decorated with small bouquets. Jean, the rector, welcomed the congregation and gave the list of hymns, which were selected by members of the organising committee. She led the service with strength and conviction, pleased that there were so many in attendance, and read selected poems by Wordsworth and Walter de la Mare emphasising the floral theme of colour. There was coffee and afternoon tea at the church during the weekend, as well as craft and plant stalls and children's activities.

The grounds of the church are part of the Living Churchyards Project. A quiet woodland area in the churchyard called "God's Pocket" was inaugurated. Intended as an oasis of peace and tranquillity, it was created by a small band of helpers with Geoff, the church treasurer and his wife. There is a bench in the sunniest spot and nesting boxes for bats. The churchyard has won the Bishop of Salisbury prize for the best overall living churchyard in Dorset several times.

Geoff and Celia came to live in the village nine years ago from Cheshire in order to be near their daughter and her family. They had been active in their church in Cheshire and have worked hard to increase the size of the local church electoral roll, among a host of things which they do to keep the building and its activities going. They live very near St Michael's, clean the interior and make sure that the grounds are well kept. They both enjoy the fellowship of the church, and participate in several events in the benefice. They have a long association with church activities: Celia's mother ran a Sunday school, and Geoff joined the church fellowship when he was a student at Oxford. Both are active in the Conservative Party, distributing leaflets, getting out the vote, and serving as tellers at elections. Geoff had practised as a solicitor prior to retirement and Celia was a clinical immunologist.

Dulcie, who is now over 90, served as a church warden and sacristan and organised the weekly flowers in church and the annual flower festival for many years. She was a primary school headteacher prior to her retirement 35 years ago. Hilary and Roger moved to the village from Sheffield via Hong Kong, where Roger had served as crown counsel for six years. He now has a private law practice in Weymouth, doing mainly criminal defence work. Hilary started as a "reading mum" in Owermoigne School, then became a full-time teacher for the reception classes. She described the former school as having "a wonderful ethos and atmosphere." Roger has been a church warden and Hilary taught Sunday school, but they are now less active in the church than they used to be.

The Rector

Jean was ordained as a mid-career priest and became rector of the Watercombe Benefice in 1999. All the congregations in the benefice are quite small, except for Broadmayne, which has a total population of over 1,000, and where the modern rectory is located. Prior to her ordination, Jean was on the agriculture faculty of Reading University. She has always been interested in farming and rural affairs, having lived in villages when she was growing up. When the Dorset appointment became available she viewed it as an opportunity to continue these interests.

Jean described herself as a "cradle Anglican". The eldest of four girls, she never realised until she went to university that women were not considered able to do all the things which men could do. Her parents had encouraged the girls to believe they could. At university, she joined the Movement for the Ordination of Women, a campaign which she thought then might last a lifetime.

Jean's initial involvement with the church was as a lay reader in South Oxfordshire where she lived. As a member of a church rural team, one of the farmers asked her, "Why do we always get such rubbish clerical appointments in the countryside?" This together with several personal faith issues encouraged Jean to begin her studies towards ordination in 1993, at a time when women were allowed to serve only as deacons. Her decision, she felt, was not only a challenge to her faith, but an uncertain career challenge at that time. But she felt that she was up for it. The ordination of women was approved by the Synod in 1992 and, after protracted debate, was implemented finally in 1994.

Her posting in the Diocese of Salisbury allowed her to follow her interests in rural affairs, but involved complicated personal arrangements, as her husband, Dudley, was a civil servant in London. She became chair of the governors of Kingston Maurward College and did some pastoral work there. She also served on the advisory committee of the Royal Agricultural Benevolent Institution. The work on rural affairs for the diocese takes about one day a week, but she is provided with some secretarial support. Her role is to bring the bishops and archdeacons together to consider countryside issues such as the fox-hunting controversy and post office closures. Through workshops and active networking she saw her role as an opportunity to create greater understanding of such issues among her colleagues. Jean became a canon and a member of the Chapter of Salisbury Cathedral in recognition of her work for the diocese.

In 2002, Jean was drafted in to help the Devon farmers during the foot and mouth disease crisis. It was a very difficult period in the South West including Dorset, as the countryside was in "lock down" from outside visitors, which had a considerable effect on the local tourist economy. The most serious problems were on dairy farms with small herds and little capital. Those who overcame the crisis were the farmers who had the capacity to reinvest, but they then faced the subsequent squeeze on milk prices. At this time, Jean felt that the people in Owermoigne and the rest of the benefice resented her commitment to activities outside the parishes which inevitably had an impact on the amount of time she had for pastoral duties. Some people in the village began to feel nostalgia for previous rectors who had no outside responsibilities to deflect them from pastoral visits.

Jean has always seen herself as a moderniser in the church. One church warden referred to her "as a bull in a china shop", in her early days in post, reflecting the rapidity of change she was seeking. Jean was seen as being very authoritative and not very keen on consultation. She was passionate about modernising church practice, including the implementation of the new liturgy which came in at the time she became rector.[3] As Richard Gregory had predicted, many

---

[3] For centuries The Book of Common Prayer, written by Cranmer in 1662, was the foundation of the Anglican service. It had become rather stilted and ritualistic in modern terms and people found it difficult to follow. To make the service more accessible, the Bishop of Salisbury rewrote it at

of the people of the village were not ready to accept either her or the changes she wished to make. The regular congregation is deeply conservative. Several felt that Jean's diary was always full with activities outside the benefice and that she was more interested in theology and the intellectual side of church practice at the expense of pastoral work. She supported the modernisation of the liturgy and the reformed Book of Common Worship. It came into use at a time when more and more women were taking up roles in the church and there was an inevitable conservative backlash against both.

Jean had always felt that in Owermoigne in particular there were mixed feelings about having a woman priest, and that the reforms were resented. The village was the least advanced in matters of liturgy, but eventually the decision to introduce the modernised liturgy was made in the benefice and the changes were implemented in the parish as well. Proposals to modernise the physical layout of the church in the village then became a great source of controversy. Jean wanted to remove the pulpit, favouring a more intimate connection with the congregation in the small church, but the congregation protested and the pulpit remained in place. The negotiation to move the altar from the back wall of the chancel to allow her to face the congregation during the benediction took five years (a change which had been introduced into the Catholic Church many years before). These issues remained a problem for her and the regular village parishioners. She recognised that her views were too

---

the request of the Synod and it became the Book of Common Worship in 2000. It includes many alternatives for different occasions and lends itself to the creation of leaflets for the use of special services.

radical for them and perhaps that they found it difficult to accept a woman in charge. Resistance to change was not confined to Owermoigne though, as it took ten years to alter the seating in West Knighton, and longer than that to agree about how to refurbish St Catherine's, Holworth.

Throughout her ministry, Jean felt that the people of Owermoigne were not hospitable or friendly towards her, which made it much harder for her to feel a sense of belonging in the village. She felt that no matter what she did, she could not put a foot right, a feeling she did not have in the other parishes. She tried to attend as many village events and activities as she could, but because of the perceived underlying resentment, it was not always a very pleasant task. She much enjoyed having a drink at the Cricket Club, and wished that some of the openness and hospitality she felt there could be transferred to church activities. Although she does the same amount of pastoral work in Owermoigne as the other villages in the benefice, she felt that people perceived that she was shirking on these activities which added to the general resentment. Despite the sociability of the village, she felt that it was not particularly friendly, a sentiment echoed by Sandra, a family counsellor, who was active in the playground dispute. Perhaps the problem is that educated women who wish to promote their views are not terribly welcome.

When the post office was closed, Jean reflected that some rural churches filled in the void and became part-time village postal services, usually together with a small café. But she felt that the suggestion would not be welcome in Owermoigne and she did not raise it. She is very interested in children and is herself a grandmother. She found her work with the schoolchildren of the village very refreshing and continued her activities at the Crossways school when the village school closed. There was an attempt to draw her into the playground dispute by the people who opposed the renovations. They requested that she approach the bishop to use the church entitlement to oppose the "construction of buildings" on what was glebe land, leased to the parish for the playground. She thought this was very strange as she favoured any refurbishment which would help the village children. Like the members of the parish council, she felt that the people in the village who opposed the scheme were property owners who were anti-young children, which was hotly denied in the heat of the debates at the time.

The Curate

Anthony Bush was ordained in Salisbury Cathedral in 2007 as a deacon. He and his wife, Philippa live in Holworth Farmhouse, a listed building from the sixteenth century which was once a rest home for monks from Milton Abbey. Anthony joined the church after he retired from the army having served as a guards officer in Germany and Northern Ireland, taught at the Staff College and did work for the MoD. Anthony and Philippa met in Malaysia where she was staying with her uncle who was Anthony's commanding officer. She was the daughter of the Bishop of Reading. Philippa has a landscape gardening business and has created a wonderful garden at their home, an imaginative creation on which both of them have worked. The family, including their daughters, ride and hunt and they have a small saddler business in Warmwell.

From 1994, Anthony had been a lay reader in Owermoigne

and Holworth. He then sought a fuller ministry, but he described the road to ordination as a rocky one. At selection, he felt that his social and army background did not stand him in good stead. He thought that his idealistic fellow candidates seemed to express rarefied views which took little account of the real world. His contribution did not go down well. His initial failure to be selected was overruled by the bishop and three months later found himself joining a course for those seeking ordination. There were several further setbacks, including initial opposition to his local appointment by Jean.

Anthony greatly enjoys his ministry and has built a good working relationship with colleagues, including Jean eventually. During his first year as a priest, he married two of his daughters. He has a strong commitment to the church, born not necessarily of a dramatic call to serve, more of a slow realisation of the hand of God moving in mysterious ways. Perhaps, he reflected, this is what his selectors initially found so difficult to accept, a process which he described as ticking boxes.

Churchgoers in the village thought that Anthony was a bit stiff to start with, but he feels now that he communicates very well with the congregation and they agree. They found the origins of his calling very familiar, he thought, and feel comfortable with it. His pet service is one of the high points of the annual calendar.

Chapter Seven

Newcomers and the Growth of the Village

Social activities in the village after 1945 included whist drives, dances and the Mothers' Union. In the village hall people gathered around a large wood burning stove. The floor wobbled and was in need of repair. The village remained quite small until new homes were built in the 1960s and 70s. The new bungalows at modest cost attracted the technicians and other staff who came to work at the Winfrith Atomic Energy Authority installation near Wool. Along the Wareham Road, the houses were more substantial and attracted professional people. Called "Piano Row," by some local people, it was assumed that the residents had pianos and were well off.

Owermoigne has never been a posh village: a few large period houses in the centre of the village are mixed with social housing and bungalow estates. Thirteen council houses in Kit Lane, the main street leading into to the village, were built just after the war (1947-1951). They are two-storey family houses with large back gardens. It was government policy at the time to have large gardens for social housing to provide some food self-sufficiency. All but a few are now privately owned but the residents tend to keep to themselves, remaining largely uninvolved in village activities.

The Origins of the Cricket Club

Owermoigne had a very active cricket team called the

Mowers which was formed in 1962 and used a field near the Mill House as a pitch for a few years: the owners, the Watmore brothers, were both keen players. They later played at Moreton. In 1963, a cricket club was founded in the old reading room adjacent to the village hall. Set up by Cecil Cree initially, it was used for Boy Scout and local NFU meetings. He had been opposed to having a pub in the village, and the local folklore has it that a pub could not be located in the village because of the well-publicised smuggling activities in the nineteenth century. The village hall committee asked the Mowers if they wanted the venue, which initially measured 3 x 4m and had no electricity or water. It was no more than a shack.

The total cost of the rebuild was £134 which was raised by selling lifetime memberships at £5. The club had a wind-up gramophone. They had to keep the premises in use in order to apply for a license. Jerry, who served several times as chair of the club built the furniture and Mike, who also served as chair, upholstered the benches. They had a paid barman for seventeen years, but in recent years it has been manned on a voluntary basis by members of the committee. From the beginning, the club sponsored special and seasonal events including quiz nights, bingo, barbeques and a Burns night dinner.

Jerry came first to Dorset from Manchester with the army and met his wife Jean at a local dance. They have lived in Owermoigne since 1961 and described those early days as full of enthusiasm for village activities. Jerry ran a youth club for several years which he started with a local policeman. From 1960-72 Jerry worked at Winfrith as an engineer. Following that he launched an animation company in Dorchester making plaster models, prior to the development of computer graphics. The youth club had about thirty local children who were taken on excursions such as swimming, fishing, ice skating and football matches. Subsequently there was no youth club for many years, which Jerry said was because of a lack of interest in village activities among young parents. This could also be because almost all families in the village now have cars to take children elsewhere to activities, combined with an avid interest in staying at home to play computer games with friends.

Pauline and her husband, Stuart, came to live in the village in 1961. Both are from the South West. Stuart was a reactor operator at Winfrith for forty years and a founder member of the village cricket team. They lived in a house with a veranda on the Wareham Road. Stuart played tennis and squash; Pauline made toys and embroidered items which she sold at craft fairs. She initially found the members of the Women's Institute very old and their activities rather boring, but gradually she and other younger incomers joined and took it over. She was twice chair and a member of the street fayre committee. With Jean, she organised the quiz nights in the village hall. In 2011 Pauline started a craft circle which meets at her home.

The Start of the Street Fayre

Jean and her husband also came to live in the village in the early Sixties. She became one of the social entrepreneurs of Owermoigne. Jean and Pauline started the street fayre, a biennial event which was very popular and well attended. It raised money for village activities and the village hall. Jean had a jam and food stall at the street fayre at Milton Abbas and together with Pauline, she brought the idea to the village in 1975. They put the idea to the village hall committee and found them to be keen.

Initially the street fayre featured local crafts and food, but soon developed into a considerable event. There was a procession including the daughter of a local farmer who was the Dairy Princess of the county, the Wessex Morris dancers and the Durnovaria Silver Band from Dorchester. Mike, a local stockman featured "Guess the weight of the prize bull". There eventually was archery, skittles, bungee jumping, pot bashing and a craft demo in the hall. Ploughman's lunches were available together with a family disco and barbeque. There were between 40 and 60 stalls and more than £3,000 was usually collected from over 2,000 visitors. The *Dorset Echo* reported it as "Villagers pull together to repair the floor of the village hall".

Activities in the Sixties

Jean always helped run village activities including the children's Christmas party and later the millennium lunch. She was the rights-of-way officer reporting to the parish council and, together with her husband, organised a village walking group. For 15 years she had a jam and pickle stall outside her home on the Moreton Road. Jean also wrote a pamphlet on the history of the village with recommended walks, which sold in the shop. She first came to the village when her husband, Herbie, who was seconded from the

Atomic Energy Authority in Cheshire to Winfrith. Eight men from the village were among its 3,000 employees. Jean said that coming from the North of England, she had to try to stop being too direct by saying what she felt in conversation. She learned that in Dorset one had to nuance what one said. She found it odd that when she called on people about village activities, she was left on the doorstep rather than invited in. In 2010, when Jean died, people were given an assurance by a neighbour in the parish magazine that her jam and pickle stall would continue. She is greatly missed and there is a photo of her in the village hall alongside the local awards for best kept village.

Jill, for years a church warden, came to the village in 1960 with her parents from another village in Dorset where her father had a farm. She and her husband, Bill, met at agricultural college at Kingston Maurward and were married after a six-year courtship. Bill's grandfather was a countryman who grew vegetables, watercress and cut flowers. His father had been a pig farmer in Throop. Jill's parents bought the Old Forge, which had become a tearoom after the last blacksmith had closed after the war. They became very active in the church and village life and started cubs, scouts and country dancing. Her mother was president of the Women's Institute and a governor of the village school.

Jill and Bill were married in St Michael's Church in 1967 and had a reception in the village hall. They were initially posted to Lincolnshire where Bill taught at an agricultural college, but they were very pleased to return to Dorset when a job came up at Kingston Maurward. They came to live in the village in 1972 in one of the cottages in the Moreton Road, initially built as farm labourers' dwellings with long back gardens suitable for family vegetable and fruit self-sufficiency. Their cottage had an old fireplace with a bread-making oven.

Bill was a founder member of the cricket team and a great enthusiast of the Cricket Club, running quiz nights and pumpkin competitions. He lectured until 1993 latterly inventing an adult course called "Computers for the Terrified". He was a mentor to many young students in agricultural management. Jill still works at the visitor's centre at the college and helps her son with the computer course Bill first developed and which he continues to teach. She organises an annual ploughing competition for the college which usually attracts fifty contestants.

Jill's church activities included the founding of the Sunday school with Anne Cree which ran for 18 years. She is secretary of the parochial parish council which meets five times a year. She has a flower stall in front of the house which is across from the jam and pickle stall. She used to put apples out when there was a bumper crop asking people to help themselves. They never did, so she decided to charge 10p for them and found that people were happier to buy them. In late 2013 Jill launched a new youth club under church auspices which initially started with pre-Christmas craft-making in the village hall.

Neighbours in Broadmayne

A similarly enthusiastic generation of people arrived in Broadmayne, a village of 500 in the early Sixties. Twenty or thirty couples, who were also connected to Winfrith, came to the village which is a few miles from Owermoigne on the road to Dorchester. June and her husband arrived from the Harwell site in Oxfordshire. They moved into a new housing estate with several other young couples associated with Winfrith. They initially found a "them and us" feeling among those long resident in the village. But it did not last. June and other women started home cooked "meals on wheels" for older people in the village in 1962. Twelve mothers who were at home with children cooked ten meals twice a week and delivered them. She explained that at the time they were not working themselves so had time for such activities, which would be much more difficult to organise today. The effort was much appreciated and helped to integrate the new young couples into village life. They joined the WI, which at the time seemed pretty boring, and began to introduce new ideas.

From the 1970s, people in Broadmayne had been keen to build a new village hall. They eventually managed to raise £64,000 and, with a matching grant from Dorset County Council, a new village hall was built in 1987. They have a drama group, a book group, dancing and sporting activities (having installed a spring floor in the village hall at considerable expense). A luncheon club was established for older people which offers a cooked lunch monthly in the hall, with people collected from home if necessary. It has proved very popular and attracts 30-35 people each time.

June chaired the Broadmayne Parish Council for forty years and founded the local history group. Broadmayne is another example of vibrant social activity on a slightly more elaborate scale, since the village population (now more than 1,000) is twice that of Owermoigne and inevitably can host a wider variety of activities. In 2009, for example, a very popular local history group was formed with small teams doing research and presentations on different themes. They have organised walks to local archaeological sites and are planning a set of publications on their work. June said, though, that the people of Owermoigne always seem much better at publicising their activities.

Growth of the Village and the Parish Plan

Newcomers to Owermoigne found homes in Chilbury Gardens built in the 1960s, with nineteen bungalows and the Hollis Mead Estate in the 1970s with eighteen houses. Social or low cost housing is still needed in the village, as young couples often have to remain with their families until housing can be found. There is preliminary talk of compulsorily purchasing the land from Hartnell Farm to build fifteen new social housing units, giving priority to people who live in or work near the village.

More recent developments in East Farm Lane (1996) and Schoolhouse Lane (2009) were projects of the Cree family with a local developer. They are tasteful village-style two storey stone houses, some with thatched roofs and small gardens, which were sold to newcomers. A few are affordable housing, managed by a housing association. The style was heavily influenced by the traditional village architectural style created by the Duchy of Cornwall in Poundbury on the outskirts of Dorchester. Although controversial, particularly in the architectural profession, Poundbury is now a very large mixed residential, industrial and commercial estate. The objective of the Prince of Wales, who inspired and built the development, was to revive an interest in traditional country and town architecture. In the 1990s, the centre of

Owermoigne, with the houses dating from the fourteenth to the eighteenth century around the church, was designated a conservation area. House prices in the village range from £130,000 for a small bungalow to £450,000 for a period house with four bedrooms. Average house prices in West Dorset are £250,000, well above the national average.

The Parish Plan

The Owermoigne Parish Plan was drawn up in 2006 at the request of the West Dorset District Council, which subsidises the activities of the parish council. Fifty-nine percent of the people in the village returned questionnaires as part of a national exercise. The greatest response (not surprisingly) came from older residents and women, who tend to find the time for such things. The parish population, which included Holworth, was 470 based on 240 houses in the village and the hamlet.

Owermoigne was considered by respondents to be a very safe place to live. The crime rate in the village is almost non-existent although people express a great fear of crime. In 2012 there were only four minor events including a caravan break-in and the theft of a bicycle. The village is a Neighbourhood Watch area and people keep a vigilant eye. Some complain that they never see a policeman in the village, but as Tony, the crime officer, who briefs the parish council on a regular basis, has often said, the number of watchful eyes on the comings and goings appears to be sufficient. Owermoigne had the highest number of suspicious incidents logged by the emergency service in the whole of Dorset. It is a village watch area and people are obviously very vigilant!

The area south of the main road, including Holworth leading to Ringstead Bay, comprises 50 per cent of the parish land, and is designated an area of outstanding natural beauty. There are several footpaths with countryside access, including the Southwest Coastal Footpath and the Hardy Way. The rights-of-way officer publishes guidelines in the parish magazine, including the designated "right to roam" areas, of which there are very few adjacent to the village, as the farmers petitioned to protect their land as working farm or grazing land. The guidelines remind people of the importance of a regard for livestock and nesting birds and the rules for dog walking.

There is a noticeboard in the middle of the village and the monthly parish magazine records activities and forthcoming events. The magazine is followed avidly, and is subscribed to by 200 households, paying £4.50 per year. It also brings news of Broadmayne and the other three villages in the Watercombe Benefice.

Replies to the Owermoigne Parish Plan questionnaire indicated that almost all the families with children in middle school and upwards have computers and broadband access, often required these days for school work. Internet access is growing rapidly even among older people. Thirty-five per cent of respondents to the questionnaire said that they listened to local radio, and about the same number read the *Dorset Echo* on a regular basis.

The village seems to be fairly evenly split between people who work part or full time (120) and those who are retired

East Farm Lane

(101). Almost all households own cars, reflecting the high level of car ownership in rural Dorset. More than half of the respondents said they use mail order services. Tesco home delivery is used by a few, although 36 per cent of respondents use internet shopping, which is growing rapidly.

The nearest GP surgeries to the village are two miles away in Crossways or in Broadmayne. Half the people in the village said they would welcome healthcare services in the village or a mobile health unit, as several have difficulty getting to the local surgeries on their own. The bus service is very infrequent; destinations are limited, and there seems to be a reduction in service year on year. There was a recent policy decision to seriously curtail local bus services, but there was a reversal of the decision, which holds at least at present. Although very few use the bus, the parish council continues to battle for a local service.

The Village Shop

From about 1860, there was a very small shop and post office in the Moreton Road which subsequently became a private home called the Old Post Office. In 1962 John Haskell opened a new village shop with a licence in Kit Lane near the entrance to the village. He had been breeding pigs in a shed behind the shop which made people somewhat concerned about the hygiene of the ham and cheese he sliced at the counter. In the 1970s a very popular couple took over, but eventually retired to Portugal. Anne, who arrived from Hertfordshire in 1972, became the postmistress, her husband and her brother managed the shop. She and her husband, an amateur jazz musician, had made the decision to strike out and move away from the family. They looked for a shop and post office in a village. As a rural postmistress, shades of *Lark Rise to Candleford*, Anne said she loved the work. She was very active in the village: treasurer of the parish council and of the WI. She thinks the village really has the same feel as when they arrived nearly forty years ago, there are just more houses. Anne has recently gone on several spectacular world cruises about which she has given afternoon presentations to the Monday Club.

The next owners of the shop were a couple from Cambridgeshire, who always dreamed of village life and having a shop of their own. The husband has been a scientist in an optical company and was known as a stalwart of pub quizzes throughout the country, particularly for his expert knowledge of military history. More usefully, his wife had managed a small supermarket. They ran the post office and shop for more than ten years, but became disillusioned by poor takings and were troubled by ill health. The task of running it became increasingly onerous and they found it difficult to hide their disappointment, an attitude which only turned people away further.

In 2007, the shop was purchased by a Dorset woman who was much more upbeat and cheerful, but after two years she put the business up for sale and moved to Perth. Her decision was not so surprising as it coincided with the closure of the post office as part of the national campaign on retrenchment of village post offices, which therefore made it difficult to sell the business simply as a shop.

Charles, an entrepreneur, reflected on this as he sat in his handsome sitting room in the Old Rectory by an open fire. He was surrounded by the antiques collected by his wife, Lynn who organised a bi-monthly antique sale in the village hall. Charles was on the parish council when the shop was put up for sale. He was told by the chair: "You are a businessman. You have the skills, see what can be done about the shop." Ninety-four per cent of the village had recorded their satisfaction with the shop, its management, stock and opening hours, in the parish plan questionnaire a few years before.

Charles approached the Plunkett Foundation, a historic name in the rural co-operative movement, which had supported many village efforts to maintain local shops that could be set up on a co-operative basis. The foundation offered a grant of £20,000 with matching funds needed to be raised by the village. Charles already had half the amount in pledges from two local people, he said. The business plan would have included the income from the rental of the small adjacent bungalow, which had been the home of the shopkeepers. Charles, who had an interest in a wind turbine company, also mooted the idea of a communally owned installation which once up and running could raise £100 per household and £7,000 per year to subsidise the shop. Fresh vegetables and fruit could be delivered in boxes from a nearby farm as an additional service. Better quality stock was considered and an internet business selling village-made goods.

"It was a lonely vigil," Charles reflected. In his final assessment to the parish council when he decided to abandon the project, he reported an exceptionally low response from village people offering to volunteer and run the shop. A significant team of about 30 would have been required, but very few responded to the call for help in the parish magazine. The Plunkett Foundation assessed the matter and felt that an enthusiastic "band of pilgrims" were simply not willing to come forward. It was proposed that each household would be asked to contribute £100 to buy shares in the project. Several had heard that projects in other villages had failed and word got around. The contribution of £100 would have posed a barrier for many.

There is a tendency to pessimism in the village which often prevails when new initiatives are suggested. In some, it has a taint of cynicism. Concerned that they might lose their share investment in the project, the idea began to sour. It is a prime example of the deeply conservative nature of the people of Owermoigne who are very circumspect, even suspicious, of major new initiatives. People in the village seem to be happy to get on with their existing activities which require no risk; major projects which pose a challenge just do not run.

The shop closed while the discussions were ongoing, and Charles felt that people began to get used to doing without it. The property remained empty for some years, but has now been converted to a private house. Without the income of a rural post office, village shops like Owermoigne's are almost impossible to sustain. Charles and his wife have moved to Italy.

Chapter Eight

Politics and the Parish Council

The Parish

The ancient parishes in England have had administrative and ecclesiastical responsibilities since the time of Elizabeth I. The formal adoption of the parish as an administrative unit took place in the sixteenth century which aided the development of a public service in the rural areas. The first effective local taxes were administered through church vestry meetings from 1601. In 1834, the Poor Law Amendment Act removed the responsibility for the poor rate to poor law unions, the origins of the present district councils.

Parish councils were formed by the Local Government Act of 1894, steered through Parliament by Gladstone against considerable opposition. Under the Act, parish councils were initially granted income from rates levied on agricultural land, but owing to repeated recessions, the funds raised was too limited and the system was abandoned. After the First World War, central government began to award additional responsibilities to parish councils, giving them authority over allotments and playing fields. The National Association of Parish Councils was formed in 1952 and became a national force, raising the profile of village governance.

The Owermoigne Parish Council is awarded about £5,600 per annum from the council tax budget. This goes on the clerk's salary, a handyman, gardener, maintenance of the bus shelters, and maintenance and insurance for the playing field. A zebra crossing on the main Wareham-Dorchester Road was promoted for about twenty years and finally appeared in 2012 paid for by council funds. The crossing connects the village with the road to Holworth.

A millennium stone, made of Portland stone, was put in place at the entrance to the village in 2001 with the name of the village carved into it. As it was the idea of a group of recently arrived young couples in the village, and not initiated by the parish council, it was instantly resented by them. The money for the project was raised at the 1999 Street Fayre. When it was put in place, some members of the parish council and others went further and vigorously criticised the selection of trees which surrounded it as "the wrong kind of trees". Some were eventually replaced. The parish council committee finally approved a small commemorative plaque to be placed on the stone.

The parish council committee has six members. They are responsible for recommendations on local planning applications to the district council. They monitor highway traffic, safety and signage, waste and refuse collection and tree conservation. Meetings are not usually well attended unless there is a planning or other issue about which people feel strongly, such as the renovation of the local garage or the development of the local garden centre, both on the main road.

Planning applications can cause problems, but are usually granted by the district council and referred on for local consideration. New building is restricted in the village because there are scarcely enough amenities (school, shop,

Election Day in the Village

post office) to qualify for expansion. This is monitored by the district council. The planning application for the renovation of the Old Forge at the centre of the village became an issue. Many of the older residents wanted it to remain the way it was. The second storey was particularly controversial, as was a brick wall in front of the house, but planning permission was eventually granted. The people who wanted to do the renovation received sarcastic notes and comments from some people, but in the end a very nice house, not at all resembling the much lamented Old Forge was built. The second storey of the new house has become a B&B.

Wendy and Peter, who have done a great deal for the church in particular, suffered great disapproval when they first decided to build a house in Owermoigne. They had come from North Warwickshire. Peter is a chartered accountant and works in publishing. Wendy worked for a number of years for the Dorset police as an administrator, and later for a local promotion company on the project to get the Jurassic Coast accepted as a World Heritage site, which was successful in 2007. They saw a plot for sale in Church Lane and decided they would build. In the course of the design process, the architect suggested that they seek outline planning permission for two houses rather than one and it was granted. But when word got around the village of their intentions, a petition raised 68 signatures against the plans for the second house. Planning permission for the two houses was granted. Peter and Wendy initially felt pretty angry about the local hostility. When people came knocking on the door asking them for help, they initially refused. But they eventually relented and offered to host an ice-cream stall in their drive for the Street Fayre. Peter has been the treasurer of the church and helps a great deal with refurbishment, as does Wendy. She set up a B&B a few years ago which has become a thriving business.

Andrew served as the chair of the parish council for many years and remains as a member; his wife, Pam, serves as the parish clerk taking care of all correspondence and circulars to and from the district and county councils and recording the minutes of the council meetings. Pam is a keen horsewoman and keeps a horse locally. Denise was a member of the parish council and runs the exercise and Pilates classes in the village hall which attract people from outside the village. She and her husband, Phil, live opposite the church in the oldest house in the village, St Michael's Cottage. They also purchased two houses next door, which are rented as holiday lets. Denise is retired from marketing caravan sites as the regional manager of Haven Holidays. Phil took early retirement as an operations officer with Channel Island Ferries. He now works as a chef in a local pub. Denise is also a keen horsewoman and keeps horses in the field next to the house.

The County and District Councils

There is a three-tier structure of rural governance: the county council and the district council each have elected members. The members of the parish council are co-opted from a list posted in the village. The County Council sets the Council Tax which is distributed to the parishes by the District Council. The village has one county councillor and two district councillors. They attend the monthly parish council meetings in the village as often as possible in rotation. One of the community police officers also attends.

David Crowhurst was the county councillor for Owermoigne for many years until his recent retirement from office. He had been a local civil servant prior to running for office as a Conservative. He represented the village for twelve years, eight of which were under a Tory-controlled council in Dorchester and four under control of the Liberal Democrats. Labour and independents have one councillor each.

Peter Stein is one of the two West Dorset district councillors. Peter was elected in 2011 and is a full-time businessman in Bournemouth working on corporate contracts mainly in the IT sector. He is a very enthusiastic Conservative councillor, covering also Crossways, Osmington, Warmwell, Poxwell and the small hamlets of Tincleton and Woodsford. He serves as a school governor and on various committees in the district and the county, which takes about twenty hours a week of his time. He enjoys using the power of networking to accomplish things.

Peter is concerned about the general lack of local involvement in political and social activities. Few members of the public attend parish council meetings' and village activities, he feels, are run by a small group of active people who often take on several roles. Although people are happy to attend activities and events, he has observed that they do not get as involved as they used to in running things. This makes it difficult to sustain activities without a renewal of people to organise them. Peter feels that the insularity of modern family life, together with home entertainment and information facilities as well as high car ownership, account for this. Things were quite different in the villages a decade or two ago, he feels.

Peter decided to run for political office because of a frustration with local governance and a wish to see more policy results. He felt, as a businessman, that more attention was needed for outcomes and the bottom line. He campaigned vigorously in the district and won the nomination at a local Conservative meeting attended by 30-40 people. He has been very involved in the recent proposals for additional house building in the district, in line with national targets for additional homes. He was pleased to have reduced by two-thirds the proposals for additional homes in Crossways, which would have trebled the current population of 2,500 and turned this large village into a town.

Crossways, two miles from Owermoigne, is not a traditional village and lacks a village centre as it was built as a series of housing estates since the war without much local character. It currently supports two shops, a post office and a health centre. Children from Crossways were bussed to Owermoigne to school until 2006, but now it is the location of Frome Valley School which serves all the primary school children of the area. Crossways also has a business park and a holiday park.

Peter said that, even though the proposals to enlarge the housing stock of Crossways were in discussion for more than a year, people ignored the potential impact until someone distributed a controversial flyer which brought seventy irate people to a parish council meeting. This, he added, demonstrated the lack of engagement until people perceived a strong local impact. The same was true of Owermoigne, which only had a few people at parish council meetings until the problem about the village playground erupted in 2009.

The Parliamentary Constituency

Owermoigne traditionally returns a large Conservative majority in district, county and parliamentary elections. With a high turnout, about 70 per cent for parliamentary elections, more than two-thirds vote Tory. Since its creation in 1885, the South Dorset constituency was held by three viscounts including Lord Cranborne, the heir to the Salisbury title and a very large landowner in the county, and other notable local families like the Hambros, the banking dynasty. The constituency includes Weymouth, now a large seaside town of 52,000, where Labour voters are able to outvote the rural parishes of the constituency, if they turn out in sufficient numbers. This can occur on a strong national swing or local issue. In 2001, Weymouth voters turned out the Conservative in favour of the Labour candidate, Jim Knight, largely because they felt that the incumbent (Ian Bruce) had not done enough to defend jobs at the Portland naval base, a historic installation established in the reign of Henry VIII.

In the 2005 election, Richard Drax, a new Conservative candidate, was elected with 45 per cent of the vote (30 per cent for Labour and 19 per cent for the Liberal Democrats). Following a long tradition of the South Dorset seat, Drax is from one of the largest landowning families in the county. The Drax family estate, Charborough Park, ten miles northwest of the village, surrounded by one of the longest brick walls in England, was established in Elizabethan times by a family which became known as Plunkett-Ernle-Earle-Drax. They were originally from Yorkshire. From 1679, there have been a six family members who became Members of Parliament, the first of whom is remembered for hosting a meeting which eventually led to the Glorious Revolution in 1688. Local lore has it that in the old days the Drax MPs could ride to Westminster without leaving their own land (denied by Richard Drax). The estate was significantly developed from the profits of sugar plantations in the West Indies in the 18th century.

Richard Drax worked the seat of South Dorset for three years prior to his election in 2010. Before he took over the estate on the retirement of his father, Richard served in the Coldstream Guards following Sandhurst. He took a course in estate management at The Royal Agricultural College at Cirencester, but initially worked as a journalist, first in Yorkshire and then as the Dorset reporter on BBC TV South for ten years. This gave ample opportunity for him to become well known in the county prior to his selection for the seat. Richard's voting record as a backbench MP is on the right of the party, particularly on immigration issues. He is a member of the backbench 1922 Committee with and often uses the rallying cry familiar to some members, "I want the country back". This anti-immigration posture would resonate with the local voters in a county which is 95 per cent white. Owermoigne itself is 100 per cent white British.

Drax is vigorously anti-Europe, although he recognises that his estate and the rest of the farms locally could not survive without subsidies from the EU. He is keenly interested in defence issues, given his military background. He regularly attends functions at the local army bases at Lulworth and Bovington, which employ several thousand local voters.

The Cree Family and Douglas Hurd at Moignes Court

Martin Cree has been the chair of the local conservatives for years, and did a great deal to boost local support for Richard Drax. There are always large posters on the entrances to his estate and surrounding farm land. Several people also have Conservative posters in their front gardens at election times. Only two people hosted Labour posters for the 2010 parliamentary election. Conservative posters dominated all the lanes and farmlands around Owermoigne. Lib Dem posters could only be found dotted around Wool, Dorchester and Weymouth.

Chapter Nine

The Village Hall and Social Life

Starting Out

The land for the village hall was donated by Captain O'Shaughnessy Cree in 1937. A retired civil servant, Miss Sheppard, lent the village the funds to build it, charging no interest on the repayment. The funds were repaid through whist drives and other activities in the hall, overseen by a retired bank manager who had a market garden on the main road. The hall is a wooden structure which has required a considerable amount of upkeep over the years. In 1972, more land was leased to the village for an adjacent car park. Heating was initially provided by a large coal stove around which people gathered for winter events; the central heating was installed in the 1980s. The original reading room, which held scout and farmers' meetings, became the Cricket Club in the early 1960s.

Detailed records of the early years reveal earnings from weddings, Conservative social occasions, dances and expenditure on tuning the piano, paraffin for heating and a children's party. From 1940 the hall was let to the War Office and used for lectures and temporary billeting of marines or engineers.

In 1945, the village celebrated VJ Day with a tea party. In 1947, electricity was installed and insurance became a regular annual item of expenditure. Among the postwar lettings were table tennis, school parties, dances and dancing classes, jumble sales and nursery classes. There were regular meetings of the Mothers' Union, the garden society and floral group, Brownies, youth clubs and whist drives.

A Wide Array of Activities

Each year a brochure of activities taking place in the hall is distributed to everyone in the village. In 2009 a village website was founded which posts the calendar of activities, a directory of clubs and organisations, special pages for the football team and the Cricket Club, and the minutes of the parish council meetings. In 2010 a soup lunch was introduced as a social event to encourage people to get together, but there were not sufficient numbers to keep it going, although the twice monthly coffee mornings with bacon sandwiches have been running successfully since then. In 2012, there was a New Year's Day walk along the coastal path attended by 20 people: a tradition established fifteen years before, organised annually by the rights-of-way officer. The skittles challenge match in January was attended by 65 people with ten teams of four players each. The tenth annual "millennium" dinner was attended by 84 people with a menu of chicken breast, vegetables and homemade pastries and cakes. There was the Royal Wedding tea in April 2011, a free family event with food prepared by village women. Commemorative mugs were presented to all the children, sponsored by local farms and businesses. About 30-40 children attended which is half the total number of under-sixteens in the village. It was organised by a committee headed by Martin Cree.

The calendar of events for 2011 included weekly Pilates and exercise classes with Denise, table tennis, short mat bowls and dog training. Monthly club meetings include the Monday club, the WI, the Flower Club, bingo and the village market. The parish council meetings and antique fair, organised by Lynn, are bi-monthly.

Annual events are the skittles challenge twice yearly with fish and chips provided from one of Daniel's shops (a local entrepreneur who lives in the village) for about 40-50, the parish council AGM, the village hall liaison meeting for all residents and the Christmas craft fair in early December. There are outdoor plant sales and lunches which raise money for local charities. In 2011, a three course "traditional Christmas lunch" in July (£8 for adults; £4 for children) raised money for the Marie Curie Cancer Centre. The hall rental is £7 per hour with a £1 discount for resident sponsors.

In 2012, there was a Diamond Jubilee lunch on 3 June for 130 people who sat down "to a banquet fit for a queen".[1] Tables were piled high with food cooked by local women. A huge jubilee cake was baked by Anne, one of the farmer's wives. The activities included quizzes, raffles, children's games and a screening of the events; £200 was raised. Peter refurbished the Victoria jubilee arch at the church and Wendy did hanging baskets in red, white and blue. A biennial open gardens scheme raised £1,000 for the flagpole, the church jubilee project (the balance going to the roof fund of the village hall).

Weekly events in 2012 added a "chubby club" giving advice on nutrition and weight management with Denise. There was

---

[1] *Compass* Parish Magazine, July 2012, p.14.

also an Olympic torch coffee morning, as the torch passed by the village. The pre-Christmas craft fair raised £420 for the Dorchester Citizens Advice Bureau. The events of 2013 were much the same as the year before.

Running the Village Hall

The village hall committee is very "hands on" – painting, cleaning, weeding the car park and putting out the furniture for events. They were described by some, though, as resistant to change when they decided not to apply for a grant to get broadband installed in the hall. The committee was chaired for ten years by Bob who retired in 2013. He and his wife came to the village ten years ago from outer London. They moved to be near their son and his family who live in Eastleigh in Hampshire. In their previous location, they had been involved in retired peoples' activities through the USA,[2] including coach trips. They wondered when they arrived if they would be accepted by the people in the village. Bob has also worked with the village football team. By 2000, the hall had become fairly dilapidated, requiring serious renovation. He has presided over considerable fund raising efforts. With the help of Dorset Community Action, which is part-funded by Dorset local authorities, they first raised £6,800 from the Heritage Lottery Fund for a new boiler and kitchen with a much needed dishwasher, providing matching funds from their reserves.

---

[2] University of the Third Age, founded by the social entrepreneur, Lord Young of Bethnal Green, the founder of the Open University. U3A runs courses for retired people.

The Village Hall

Earnings for the hall come from rentals and a £1,000 contribution annually from the Saturday market stalls, which have now been running for more than ten years. In 2012 the hall required re-roofing and painting inside and out at a cost of £26,000. The Heritage Lottery Fund provided £10,000 with matching funds from the reserves and a contribution from the Dorset Community Association. This left £11,000 in reserve. Some members of the committee wanted to raise the hourly rental cost, but Bob opposed it. When Bob retired, he left the hall in much better shape than when he took over ten years before. He has said that there is a problem finding people to serve on the committee and described the local people as three types: volunteers, supporters and the non-engaged.

Although it has been noted that class or status distinctions in Owermoigne are relatively muted, people who live in social housing in the centre of the village rarely participate in local events and activities. The twelve houses were initially built for farm labourers but were no longer needed. Farm work is now done largely by seasonal contractors who live elsewhere. Several of the families were settled in by Dorset Council rather than choosing to live in the village, and remained reticent about joining anything or taking part in local activities. They were said to have the view "if the activities do not benefit me, I am not interested." When a playgroup was started by two local mothers in the 1980s, the children from these houses had to be collected and returned by one of the mums in charge. Only at the time of the playground dispute did the people from the council houses join in, as they had several young children. They attended meetings and made their views known. Most people feel that their lack of interest in village activities is more a question of their social outlook and family psychology than class distinction.

The work of Bob on the village hall committee is ably supported by Val who came to the village twelve years ago. Val has now taken over as chair. She and her husband moved to the village because she was attracted by information about the activities in the village. Val had been looking for a place to become active in the community. Owermoigne has now become their longest residence in a single place. They previously lived for five years in army accommodation while her husband was in the service. She described the life as a closed community of army wives but she enjoyed the togetherness. When they moved to Ferndown (a suburb of Bournemouth), while continuing to work at Bovington as civilian employees, they felt they did not get to know anyone except their nearest neighbours.

As a child growing up in Swindon, Val's family lived in the old town of railway cottages: "Everyone knew one another: it was like a village." They enjoyed family holidays in Weymouth which she always remembered fondly. When she and her husband settled in to their new home in Owermoigne, she joined the WI and organised the raffle at the Saturday market. When she stopped working a few years thereafter, she had more time and became secretary of the village hall. She enjoys using the skills she learned at work to produce brochures and flyers for events, place notices in the parish magazine and make contact with the local press. Val organises the village bingo each month and helps June organise the pre-Christmas craft fair, the proceeds of which last year went to Dorset Air Ambulance. Val's husband does not like serving on committees, but helps out moving tables and chairs for events when needed and doing minor repairs on the building

Val served on the committee of the Royal Wedding tea and suggested to Martin that the event should be free entry (as she had remembered events from her childhood) so funds were raised to sponsor the event. Val was in charge of the jubilee lunch. They asked each person to bring a contribution of prepared food. They had a list of dishes required and went from house to house asking people if they wished to attend and what they wanted to contribute. There were many items which were deliberately quite inexpensive to prepare, for families of limited means who wished to attend; 120 people attended. Some people recalled their childhood street parties for former royal occasions. A fund at the parish council made a donation of £80 for decorations and children's' gifts.

Frank, a retired businessman from Oxfordshire, was on the parish council and chair of the village hall prior to Bob. He said that he got fed up with the sceptical attitude of people towards new ideas and found them a bit old fashioned and out of touch. He retreated to the more solitary pursuits of model boats and computer flight simulations. He and his wife became active in Probus, the business and professional retired peoples' association in Weymouth, with about fifty members.[1] They both became officers and helped organise lunch outings, excursions and speakers and found that they enjoyed much more social resonance with other members than they felt in the village. They subsequently moved elsewhere.

---

[1] Founded in the UK in 1965, it is now a worldwide network.

The Women's Institute and the Saturday Market

The Owermoigne Women's Institute was founded in 1945. Current activities include a speakers' programme with lectures on such subjects as antiquarian book dealing, historic musical boxes, war memorials in the county, local history and local memoirs, holiday travel and a demonstration on how to make marzipan fruits. Regular luncheon club events at local restaurants are very popular. At each monthly meeting they have a competition such as decorated eggs or decorated baked goods. They organise outings to places like Sherborne Castle. Fundraising activities such as cream teas donate their proceeds to the village hall. About half the funds raised annually go to the National Federation of Women's Institutes.

The chair of the WI is Betty, the quintessential social entrepreneur in the village. Betty was the inspiration behind the launch of the monthly village market, and the Monday Club, both of which have been a huge success. She was nominated as a community champion in a competition organised by West Dorset District Council. Betty was also one of the moving spirits behind the WI History of Owermoigne which was published in 1986. Prior to their arrival in the village, Betty and her husband worked at Cliff House, a boys' boarding school for children with special educational needs, located in Tincleton, a few miles from the village. Betty's husband was the deputy head and she acted as the matron. There are boys who still keep in touch. They lived in a cottage in the grounds with their three children.

The school was a stately home purchased by Dorset County Council in the 1950s. It was later sold as it was deemed too expensive to maintain as a school.

Betty is originally from Exeter and her husband from Sheffield. While they were working at Cliff House, they bought a weekend cottage in Broadmayne with a small garden. Someone advised them that there was a house in Owermoigne with a big garden for sale. Bill was a keen gardener and they bought the house. Betty said that people might not have been so forthcoming to be interviewed for this book in the first years that they knew the village. She found them secretive and uncooperative. She joined the WI shortly soon after coming to live in the village and has been the president for many years.

The idea for the village market project came from similar events in Broadmayne and Wool, where some of Betty's baking had been on sale. She became aware that the village hall needed money for refurbishment, so from the outset an arrangement was established to give a certain percentage of earnings to the hall. The stalls in the village market include cakes and pastries, crafts, garden plants, vegetables, books, bric-a-brac. Coffee, tea and biscuits are served.

June does the craft stall in Owermoigne and in the Wool weekly market as well. She knits and embroiders and decorates linens with Dorset feather stitch. She makes paper crafts and jewellery, all at very low prices. June met her second husband at the tea dance at the Corn Exchange in Dorchester. He was from Portland and a keen gardener. He visited June's garden when it was opened for the National Gardens Scheme. He took a saxifrage plant and when they got together (at the prodding of their respective daughters), he brought it back from Portland and planted it in her garden.

June is a church warden and opens and closes the building each day. She had been an active member in the village horticulture society which was popular and ran for many years. June is the daughter of a dairyman who settled in Dorset when she was three years old. They were poor, but she enjoyed a very happy childhood, able to roam freely with her young friends. When first married, she worked as a clerk for a corn and feed merchant. They could not get a council house so they lived with her parents. Eventually they were given a wartime Nissen hut in West Knighton with breeze-block walls and a corrugated-iron roof. They lined the walls with newspapers and painted over them. Her husband had a JCB and worked for the area gas board. They finally got a council house where they raised their three children. She then worked as a shop assistant in Goulds Department Store in Dorchester, eventually working her way up to be a buyer of silver plate and crystal.

Ann is a member of the village hall and WI committees, helps organise bingo and other activities in the village hall and does weekly flower arrangements for the church. She has worked in a care home in Dorchester, but mainly does housekeeping and cleaning for people in the village now. She originally came to the village from Dorchester in 1974 with her first husband who was a dairyman on the estate. Two years later he contracted brucellosis and could no longer work around cattle. They left Dairy Cottage and were moved to a council house in Kit Lane, where she still lives. With her

Selling Plants at the Saturday Market

second husband, Rob, a self-employed painter, they bought the house. Rob works for people in the village and did the refurbishment of the village hall. He is a keen collector of recorded rock music (and very knowledgeable about it), buying discs at local markets and selling them on eBay all over the world. Ann cooks Sunday lunch for an elderly widower in his 80s. She also stocks his freezer for the week, so he can microwave the meals. She is constantly busy and often goes to the Dorchester market on Sunday and to car boot sales, sometimes setting up a stall to sell. In the Saturday market, Ann has the bric-a-brac and book stall. She also attends the Monday Club and has been celebrated for her stories of her childhood in Dorchester and her early married life in the village, very popular when there are member presentations.

The Monday Club

Susan and Beth started the Monday Club at the prompting of the village hall committee. They were looking for additional activities to fill the hall on slow days and to involve more men in local activities. Susan and Beth distributed a flyer to all the houses in the village asking what ideas people had for new activities and events. The Monday Club was formed as a fairly casual group with no constitution or elected members. Sue, the treasurer, keeps the proceeds in a biscuit tin rather than a bank account, as they have no constitution and are not therefore legally formed. Annual membership is £10 or £1.50 per session. Betty is the honorary chair; Beth is the secretary. Many talented and active older people in the village do not use computers or the internet. Sue and her husband Tony do voluntary computer support for people in the village. Age Concern has run a course on computing in the village hall.

Beth and her husband Alex moved to the village in 1995 from Twickenham and after coming for weekends, they decided to settle permanently. Prior to retirement, Alex owned a garage and Beth did personnel management. When they initially came to the village they were looking for activities in which to become involved. They started with an ice-cream stall at the Street Fayre in traditional costumes, as their house is on the main street near the church. Beth has served as the treasurer of the village hall committee. They attend church regularly. They found it a bit odd when others told them shortly after arrival that the congregation had to wait for the Cree family, who always sit in the front pew, to leave before the congregation filed out. They regarded that as a relic of the past. Beth said that they think living in the village is wonderful.

The Monday Club distributes an annual brochure with their activities, planned a year ahead. They have had speakers on local history and Dorset folk songs, home watch and security, Thomas Hardy and William Barnes, the history of Kingston Maurward College, growing watercress, fitness and many other topics. They have a Christmas lunch at a local restaurant and have organised local outings to Tyneham, Lulworth Castle and the Tank Museum at Bovington. Several times a year, they have a members' own session, when people tell life stories of childhood, hobbies, travels and other topics of interest. On a cold wet winter afternoon, it served as very popular entertainment and was remarkably jolly. It is a way for people to share reminiscences and an opportunity to look for common threads and get to know one another better. Most are a generation marked as children or young people by the war. The men tend to talk about army experiences, but the women members share a wide variety of life experiences, complaining the while that they are most unaccustomed to public speaking. Some like Ann have been asked often to continue their popular reminiscences.

Jean spoke about a rural childhood in Cheshire where the children were free to roam and even went boating in a borrowed punt from the manor house until they were caught. They ran back and forth during the harvest waiting for a ride on the haywain. They earned pocket money during the potato harvest. Jean saved for a pair of ice skates, as the village pond froze in winter. Her mother had been an accomplished seamstress and Jean learned to make all her own clothes.

The "Horty", Horticultural Club

This was one of the earliest clubs in the village, founded more than forty years ago but it was disbanded in 2011 owing to lack of support. In 2009, the club hosted spring and summer shows with competitions in different categories of plants and blooms. They had a lecture on thatching and visits to gardens. But there was a dwindling number of people to go on outings: previously over-subscribed in coaches, they found that they could barely fill a mini-bus. Above all, there was dwindling interest in serving on the committee and plan future events. Dorset Record Office took the archive of the club and the assets were divided among two RHS charities – the Benevolent Society for Retired Gardeners and the Children's Gardening Project and two favourite local charities – the Dorset Air Ambulance and the Weldmar Hospice in Dorchester. Their book collection was sold, and show materials were passed on to the Owermoigne Flower Club. They rounded off the final meeting with mulled wine and biscuits and a promise to keep in touch.

The Flower Club

Formed in 1978 by the members of the "Horty" who were interested in flower arranging, a recent AGM was attended by 40 people. The Flower Club is a local chapter of a national organisation and has 75 members from the five villages of the benefice which meet in the Owermoigne village hall. Throughout the year, they have demonstrations of seasonal arrangements on imaginative themes. One theme, on famous people, included arrangements inspired by Charles Rennie Macintosh, Kate Moss, Vivien Westwood and Marilyn Monroe. One lecture on the popular subject of the positive qualities of weeds pointed out that dandelions have more Vitamins A and C than any other vegetable; that chickweed and nettles are often used in salads by herbalists and that there is recent research on turning weeds into bio fuel. One member showed slides from a trip – gardens in South America. The recent competition was "A Day at the Seaside". They have hosted lectures on gardens such as Monet's in Giverny, France, organised visits to gardens and sent entries to local flower festivals.

Hobbies and Neighbouring Activities

Walking and birdwatching were among the most popular village activities, according replies to the 2006 Owermoigne Parish Plan questionnaire. Dick is one of the village's most expert birdwatchers. With the permission of local farmers, he has taken some stunning photos of nightjars, Dartford warblers and water birds including lapwings, snipe and curlews. At Holly Farm, he has photographed barn and tawny owls. Alfie, the owner of Holly Farm, he said, was good about maintaining the trees and hedges for the wildlife. In the woodlands he has seen buzzards, sparrow hawks and kestrels. In addition to the local sika, fallow and roe deer, there are two badger sets near the village. Dick has lectured in the village hall with his slides.

The "crafts and chatter" group meets weekly in the winter months in Pauline's home. People are encouraged to bring their favourite craft "and have a natter, a cuppa and learn something new". Among the crafts are knitted frilly scarves, embroidery, patchwork, felt animals, paper craft and quilting. Some of these are sent to local children's charities.

Barbara and David moved to the village from Cornwall in 2006. They are members of the Royal Dorset Yacht Club and have a cruising yacht. In the summer months they sail to the French coast with fellow members. They spent a great deal of time refurbishing their large garden. Barbara did learning support at Kingston Maurward College helping students aged16-plus with spelling and maths problems. David is an engineer who developed an early electric car. He now works for BMW in Munich and they have settled there.

Suzanne and her husband come from London. They initially came to Dorset to refurbish a boat: "I spent my courtship sanding a boat in Poole Harbour," she said. Her husband, Mike is an accountant, so they found it easy to resettle. He works in Weymouth and was the Cricket Club treasurer for several years. Suzanne is a keen gardener and has two

Tawny Owl at Holly Farm

daughters. She reflected that it would be difficult to live in the village without two cars, especially given children's after-school and weekend activities. And this would be very hard on a low income family because the public transport is so poor.

David is a very keen cyclist, who was brought up in Weymouth. He worked in the police service in what was Northern Rhodesia. On his return to the UK, he joined the probation service and settled in Broadmayne. His wife, Eve, was born in Jerusalem, the daughter of an army officer. When she and her parents returned to Britain after the end of the mandate in 1948, they were given a bombed out house in Sidcup, Kent, but eventually were moved to a housing estate in Essex (with granny to increase their points towards resettlement). When they married they got a tandem bike. David is a member of the Cyclists' Touring Club which is over 100 years old. He does a great deal of long-distance cycling. Despite serious health problems in recent years, Eve has a remarkable attitude to life and fun. They are planning lots of travel with their motor home. They bought a house in the Charente several years ago and have been learning French. Eve and Anne are members of the Crossways handbell ringers who perform in the church on occasion. They also play at summer fetes, hospitals, and retirement and nursing homes.

"The Owls", Owermoigne's Football Club

The teenagers of the village attend the Thomas Hardye School in Dorchester, which is named after a merchant adventurer and smuggler who endowed the first school in Dorchester in 1597 (perhaps a distant ancestor of the more well-known Thomas Hardy). The school has 2,500 pupils and 300 staff. The village had a football team before the war, but it became very lively in the Sixties together with the cricket team. The team was relaunched with local teenagers in 2007. Bob, the former village hall chair, was instrumental in this. They are described on the village website as "an ambitious but friendly group of players..." They play in the Dorset third division and have often appealed for local land on which to play, but still play on the field at Crossways. Sponsorship was raised to provide a kit for each of the players in the senior league of 16-18 year olds. The parish council provided a donation of £600. Contributions have also been made from village hall activities and sponsorship from local businesses has also helped. The lads did fund raising at the Street Fayre while it lasted.

The Street Fayre

Graham chaired the Street Fayre for ten years. He and his wife who lived in Hertfordshire for more than 30 years came to live in the village in 1998 when the houses in East Farm Lane were built. They remember a welcoming wine and cheese party for the newcomers which "felt like a 'freshers' tea," they said. Beryl, who was a headteacher before retirement, joined the Flower Club. She is also in the Briantspuddle Singers with fifty members in a nearby village, practising weekly and giving several concerts a year, mainly of oratorio music.

Graham edited the National Trust newsletter for Dorset for ten years. He became treasurer of the "Horty". As a retired marketing executive from ICI, his management and organisation skills were quickly recognised in the village. In the ten years that Graham was head of the biennial village fayre, there were about 1,000 visitors to the event. From the proceeds, £3,600 was distributed to village clubs and societies, the church and the school in almost equal shares of £400.

By 2007, Graham felt that someone else should take over as the event took the best part of a year in preparation. He felt that fresh ideas were needed. The looming problems about the village playground partly influenced his decision, as he felt that the village could not mount another large event given the fractious atmosphere at the time. Others have said that the real problem was that no one would come forward to take over the role of chair. Its cancellation was a great loss of income for all the village activities. Some complained that people were not notified that the event would not continue without a new chair, and of lack of support. Might it have survived? There was a committee in place, but no leader. Carol, the secretary, said that Graham was excellent at managing and administering the event, but it would be difficult to replace him. Many rural village fairs, that begin life as a local events with local produce and handmade goods, often morph into a more commercial event if popular, with outside stallholders who follow such events as an opportunity for extended selling. This was the case in Owermoigne. There were always problems parking cars for so many visitors and the proposed expansion of the playground into the area customarily used added to the problems.

When he resigned, Graham and Beryl began to look for activities outside the village and joined Probus and became officers. They tried to learn Italian and French with the U3A but found the teaching very amateur. "Focus on Finance", also a U3A activity, was run by an ex-tax specialist who formed an investment club of twenty people: that was more interesting and useful.

Owermoigne Street Fayre, 2007

<u>Activities</u>
Guess the weight of the lamb (in the Glebe Field)
Stocks (for photos)
Face painting and hair braiding
Finger painting
Coconut shy
Badge making (machines hired)
Horseshoes
Punch and Judy
"Bowl the pig"
"Bash a rat"
Roulette wheel
Raffle

<u>Village Stalls</u>
Silent auction
Tombola
Morning coffee
"Meet Norrie Woodall"
Soft drinks
Bric-a-brac

Arts and crafts exhibition

19 bookings for commercial stalls

<u>Entertainment</u>
Town crier
Morris dancers
Wessex military band

<u>Marquee</u>
Ploughman's lunch
Cream teas

Gross income: £5,372
Expenditure: £1,679

The Cricket Club

There are about 130 members of the village drinking club founded in 1962 in a small building next to the village hall. Membership is open to people in the village at now £10 per year. The drink is considerably cheaper than in a pub. There are about thirty regulars who use the club frequently and have become a friendship network. There was originally a full time steward in the club, but since custom fell away and wages rose, the bar has been manned on a co-operative basis by members of the Cricket Club committee.

Mike was a long standing chairman until 2009, after which there was a succession of people who took over running the club with the committee. But both the management and the popularity of use were in decline. The committee are always looking to recruit new members, but the constitution prevents them from recruiting more than 20 per cent from outside the village. From the parish magazine, a plea for help was published:

Street Fayre

Street Fayre, Guess the Weight

> *The committee has been working at full stretch this year and we desperately need new members or restructured opening hours will have to be considered. At least two of the members of the committee are standing down.*
> *Please let us know if you would like to join us. The reluctance of members to help with the running of the club has burnt out committees past and present and the future of the Club is in the balance if this situation is not addressed, so please, many hands make light work, we need more help.*[1]

In March 2013, the club secretary updated the following:

> *Hopefully the black eyes, broken noses and bruises are all healing nicely in the aftermath of the AGM. The Club has repaired all the furniture and windows and replaced the bottles broken in the spaghetti western style bar brawl that was our Annual General Meeting...*[2]

This was apparently a spoof aiming to attract attention to the problems the club was facing. The AGM was in fact very poorly attended.

Annual events of the Cricket Club on a seasonal basis are:

January
Burns Night supper with music by a local band

February
Valentine's wine and cheese party

---

[1] Alan, Hon Sec. of the Cricket Club, *Compass*, November 2011, p.11.
[2] Ibid, p. 17

March
St Patrick's Day celebration

April
Easter Egg draw and family evening in fancy dress Easter bonnet parade
Quiz Night

May
Bank holiday barbeque
"The sun actually smiles down long enough for members and guests to sit outside, chomp on their burgers, and enjoy the musical entertainment."

June
"Vinyl night", old fashioned disco Quiz night
Solstice walk followed by ploughman's lunch

July
Fourth of July night with local boogie woogie pianist, Ben Waters

September
"Videoke" night

October
Annual pumpkin growing competition Halloween fancy dress with wine and cheese

December
Christmas Bingo
Christmas Quiz and Party Carol Singing
The Club is open all day on Christmas and Boxing Day.

The Cricket Club 1

The Cricket Club 2

In April 2013, Ian took over as chair of the club. He grew up in Owermoigne and played for the cricket team from the age of 13. He and his family moved away from the village in the 1980s and he now lives in Corfe Mullen, about thirty-minutes drive to the east. He works for Barclays International in Poole. But he had always kept in touch with the club and has attended often. He stepped into the breach when there was no one to take over as chair from his friend Jim. The club has had a new lease on life since Ian took over. There had been a lack of support and interest, even from the committee. Among the problems was a lack of agreement about the future of the club: some wanted it to be a rather exclusive wine bar to entertain golfing friends, but Ian and the others continued to support a mixed set of events.

The committee makes the decisions about events by majority vote. Ian believes that his role is to put these decisions into action, not try to interfere in decision-making. Previous chairs of the club had been rather autocratic, but that is not how he sees his role. Enthusiasm has been renewed even in the first months after he took over in the spring of 2013. He found that an increase in turnover was needed and began to tighten up the ordering of stock and running the club in a more business-like manner. The club has never been in debt, but always needs to have reserve funds for refurbishment of its old premises. There is talk of building a conservatory at the back to enlarge the indoor drinking space. Shortly after the club was founded in 1962 a tree fell on the small building and nearly demolished it. When the refurbishment was complete, they used the timber from the tree to rebuild the bar itself.

Chapter Ten

Dispute and Peace Restored

For three years from 2006, the number of children in the village became a serious political issue.[1] The Parish Plan of that year had suggested that there were not enough activities and playground equipment for children, who seemed to meet at each other's houses and ride their bikes around the lanes of the village. There were swings and a roundabout on glebe land above the village. It was a small limited play area, not much used.

A report to the parish council in September 2006 indicated that funds could be raised for new playground equipment through the Dorset Community Association.[2] The Owermoigne Youth Quest (OYQ) was founded with a mission statement referring to the well-being of children in the village. Fundraising events were planned and estimates for equipment were sought. The OYQ (known in the village, rather unfortunately as the "Oik") were initially very ambitious, noting that grants up to £60,000 were available for playground equipment. A cycle path was to be included in the scheme, which was approved by the parish council. They had supported the playground renewal project from the start.

---

[1] The NHS Register for that year registered 90 children under the age of 16, communication from the chair of the parish council, 2010. But this was hotly disputed by those who opposed the new playground equipment.
[2] A charity funded by the EU and Rural District Councils in England, the DCA has projects throughout Dorset.

The initial proposal for equipment included building equipment for young children, but it was also looking for structures to engage the teenagers of the village. This included an "alien", a brightly coloured metal tower with chutes, slides and ropes. The large structure would be visible from Church Lane, the main street of the village, and that is where the problems began. Residents in sight of it objected to the height and mass of the structure and asked why the OYQ had not considered more tasteful wooden equipment which had been used in other local village playgrounds.

There was a proposal for a small shed or clubhouse for older children, frowned upon by some parents, as they were not certain what their children might be up to out of sight. The detractors seized on this and raised the issues of smoking, drugs and under-age sex. Building such facilities had become controversial elsewhere. The objectors were delighted to discover an instance where such a clubhouse had been demolished following the intervention of the Thames Valley Police on several occasions and the growing opposition of local people. The firm which sold the equipment and promoted the idea of youth shelters, as they were known, published a warning to local areas considering it:

> *Don't do it without clearly identifying the local problems and ensuring that the young people want it. Make sure that the nearest residents support it.*

The dispute began and overwhelmed relationships, activities and the whole atmosphere in Owermoigne for three years.

Duncan, who chaired the OYC promoters, was accused of

being arrogant and dismissive of the opponents. He and the supporters were charged with vagueness about the actual plans and not answering questions clearly at public meetings. They were stunned by the vociferous opposition to the playground scheme, especially as it had been supported by the parish council. The proposers felt that they had right on their side as they were "doing it for the children". They accused the middle-class residents of Church Lane who objected of being concerned only with their property values. They also accused them of selfishness and being unconcerned about the welfare of the village children, a charge which they hotly denied.

Open meetings were held in the village hall which pitted neighbour against neighbour – in some cases between people who had known one another for almost a lifetime. People were very rude to others and some were told to "shut up!" It was deeply unpleasant. There was no dialogue. Some of the young mothers who supported the scheme were moved to tears by the acrimony of the opposition. Duncan was threatened by one of the property owners that "he would ruin his local building business" unless they stopped the plans.

The planning application process for the playground project to West Dorset District Council became the theatre for the enflamed feelings on both sides. The council planning committee must have been stunned, and the matter was initially deferred. The chair of the parish council might have tried to diffuse the situation by inviting people to discussion and debate, but he seemed swept away by events, never having envisaged the bitterness the playground plans would provoke. There was record attendance at all the parish council meetings throughout 2007. The chair and other members of the parish council inevitably stood by their decision to support the scheme. They deeply resented the opposition of property owners. The playground was on glebe land, but managed and maintained by the parish council. Charles, who owned the rectory adjacent to the proposed new playground resigned after being a very active member with many new ideas. One opponent actually approached the rector to ask her to take the matter up with the diocese, but she refused.

The OYC continued to raise funds for the project, receiving a donation from the county council and sponsoring a local fashion show and carol singing. Such events were studiously ignored by those in the village who opposed the project, but they still attracted considerable support. The OYC applied for large grants but eventually were only able to raise a small portion of the funds they sought and presented a revised plan. In the meanwhile, some activities for the children about wildlife and the environment were started by Sandra in the village hall. They ran for a few years but were not necessarily well attended. All such efforts compete with much more compelling computer games and online activities of local children. The effort did not endure.

Until the spring of 2009, the atmosphere in the village remained poisonous. People seemed to be going over and over the issues, recounting in great detail new information or conversations with people. There seemed to be nothing else so prominent on the village agenda. With the issue still smouldering, neighbours were not talking to one another and turned away when they passed each other on the lanes of the village. The Street Fayre which should have taken place in the summer of 2009 was a major casualty. The OYC had asked for a contribution from the 2007 event when the proceeds were distributed, but the committee refused on the basis that they did not take part in the planning and did not participate in the event. The battle lines had been drawn.

Eventually the project was reduced to a much more modest upgrade of the playground including new swings and a zip wire (much loved by my grandchildren when they visit). Planning permission for the more substantial equipment which was in the original proposal was eventually obtained, but the fundraising efforts did not materialise. The people who live next to the glebe field and had rented it for years for grazing horses, purchased it in 2010 when it was put up for sale by the diocese for £100,000. They were staunch opponents of the playground scheme. The deed contained a covenant which required the landlord's permission for anything in the upper field where the playground is located. That seemed to seal its fate in legal terms.

Things began to simmer down; neighbours made tentative efforts to renew contact. Most activities in the village were largely unaffected. People said, "I don't think the village is the same since the dispute." One person agreed and added that "it had left some dirt on the wall." (2013)

The Players

Duncan and his wife moved to the village in 1997. They have three children. Both were involved in village activities, including the millennium stone and the Street Fayre. Alison has served on the parish council. "We had great pride in the village and wished to be involved," she said. Their grown children had local jobs in the garden centre and the caravan park. They were deeply surprised by the hostile reaction of some in the village to the renovation of the playground. The vehemence of some people continued for another year or two; people who passed their garden sometimes took the opportunity to made nasty personal comments.

Tessa and her husband moved from West Knighton, where they had raised £50,000 for a new playground, much admired by all. It was in rustic timber and held to be a model for what might have been favoured in Owermoigne, although the equipment was mainly for young children. Tessa and her husband bought a piece of land on the Wareham Road and lived in a caravan for a while until they finished building the house. From her experience, she knew how to initiate the applications for funds and the planning process. She was thus an essential part of the OYC. Tessa had managed her own shoe design company previously and she said that she had more business skills than some of the others involved. She did not really wish to become too involved, but saw the gaps in what they were doing and continued to support them.

Charles and Lynn at the Old Rectory already had experienced difficulties with damage to the perimeter wall and bottles and other rubbish thrown over into the garden from the play area. On the basis of a letter of protest Charles sent to the OYC, he was threatened with legal action which prompted his resignation from the parish council. He and the other protestors were pleased when the Dorset Wildlife Trust found bats in the playground field with several rare species, which delayed the project while bat boxes were installed (cut by Duncan and put together and installed by the children).

Pat lives in Dairy Cottage in Church Lane, one of the oldest thatched houses in the village in full view of the field where the playground is located. Pat had been a schools inspector in Liverpool. She started out as a PE teacher in Wales and growing up in the Rhondda gave her the idea of seeking to live in a village in her retirement. She felt that the meetings about the playground became very acrimonious principally because the OYC people provided little concrete information about their plans. She felt that the proposed structures, particularly the "alien" were outlandish for a village like Owermoigne. "There had been a vigorous debate about the tree planting around the millennium stone, as some thought that the wrong sort of trees had been chosen, but it was nothing like this!" It had been the most bitter debate in the village in living memory, but eight years on it is a faint memory.

Chapter Eleven

Holworth People

People in Holworth live in two places: scattered along a hillside overlooking Ringstead Bay, Weymouth and Portland or further inland in a hollow which once housed the monks of Milton Abbey. They are adjacent to the cliffs of White Nothe on the Dorset coastal path, maintained by the National Trust. A fourteenth-century barn, also owned by the trust, is in the contour of the adjacent rolling farmland and still in use by a local dairy farmer. Holworth House, which is 150 years old, is the most prominent of the coastal residences.

The people of Holworth love living in this isolated, spectacular location. For them, it is an important life choice, although it is a long way from the nearest shop or garage. And in winter there is a strong onshore wind along the track which runs along the top of the cliff through a National Trust car park. It can be treacherous and is the only access to the outlying houses on the coast. The access to the track is through a five-bar gate which is closed to other motor vehicles.

Anthony and Philippa live in the oldest house, Holworth Farmhouse, which formed part of the monks' residence, abandoned in the seventeenth century. Anthony has been mentioned earlier as the curate in the parish. The early history of Holworth, Holverde in the Domesday Book, is described in chapter one. It is thought that the name is Saxon, meaning enclosure or hollow. The people in Holworth are drawn together by both their life choice to live there and the need to maintain and protect their small chapel of St Catherine's, a timber structure overlooking the sea.

"Burning Cliff"

The dwellings on the lower part of the hill have always been subject to erosion. The original ones were fishermen's cottages. In the *Gentleman's Magazine* in May 1827 there was a meticulous account of the loss of more than thirty feet of land and a cottage owned by Baggs, a fisherman, who with his family had prudently evacuated in 1815. The purpose of the article was to describe in detail a natural phenomenon of an oil shale fire in the area in 1826. It was started by heat generated by the decomposition of iron pyrites, a common element in bituminous shale. It flamed along 650 feet of the surface throwing up columns of "dense suffocating smoke" and became a site of local interest near the coast. Blueish flames rose high into the air, visible from Weymouth. Public curiosity was aroused; some were worried about living near a volcano.

It continued to burn for several years. The *Gentleman's Magazine* described it thus: "a curiosity of the learned as well as the unlearned, eager to dive into the workings of nature induced them to apply pick axes to portions of rock in order to ascertain the cause of this wonderful phenomenon which after all efforts proved fruitless. Nature in her operations proved too subtle and impenetrable for human ingenuity to uncover her designs." There is shale all along this coast with substantial deposits at Kimmeridge Bay heavily exploited 150 years ago. The area might be of interest to the current fracking industry, but it is likely to escape as a protected area of exceptional natural beauty. The fire eventually burned out.

St Catherine's Church

Dr Robert Linklater, a prebend of St Paul's Cathedral, bought Holworth House in 1887 as a holiday home. He used to send a token "tythe" of prawns to the Vicar of Milton Abbey, keeping alive an old legacy of monastic days. Adjacent to the house, there was an oratory in which Dr Linklater held regular services. After his death in 1915 the oratory was closed. In 1926 his widow built a new wooden chapel on a lovely site along the coast, just below the house. On her death in 1942, she left a legacy to the Linklater Trust for the upkeep of the St Catherine's. The small churchyard contains few graves, but is a cherished resting place reserved for Holworth people. Only those who live in the hamlet are permitted to hold weddings or baptisms in the chapel or be buried in the grounds. The graveyard does include a few bodies washed up from the sea within the parish boundaries. Until 1954, the hamlet remained an ecclesiastical parish of Milton Abbey, although today it is in the parish of Owermoigne and the Watercombe Benefice.

St Catherine's is visited in summer by passing ramblers and other day trippers. The congregation annually welcome a holiday adventure team of children from inner London. Attendance at summer services is often very large. There was a special service for the Olympics in August 2012 attended by many: the sailing competition in Weymouth Bay was visible from the site.

The church has a beautiful etched glass window by Laurence

Whistler, who also did all the windows in Moreton church when it was rebuilt after the war. The exterior is clad with cedar tiles, the floor and interior walls are of wood. For a long time there were discussions and some heated controversies about the refurbishment of the fragile structure of the church. Funds were available from the Linklater Trust. But the protracted discussions served as another example of how long it takes to accomplish anything in rural parishes. Finally by 2010 a plan had been agreed and the church, sometimes unjustly described as "little more than a garden hut", was restored. New doors were opened seaward bringing in more light and the seating was increased from 35 to 45. In the summer and for special events a canopy is erected on the seaward side to accommodate a larger congregation.

Holworth House

The house was built in the mid-nineteenth century on the site of earlier buildings. The two old mullion windows in the oratory are older and almost certainly came from elsewhere. When Dr Linklater's widow died in 1926 the house was sold to Jack Churchill, the younger brother of Winston, also as a holiday home. Often referred to as the more famous Winston's "secret brother", Jack rated scant mention in his extensive autobiography. And despite having offered considerable help with his book on their father, Randolph Churchill, his contribution was never acknowledged. In a boyhood incident on holiday in Switzerland, Jack is simply referred to as "the other boy". He seemed to have been airbrushed out of history.[1] Despite local rumours, Winston

---

[1] Adam Roberts, "Winston Churchill: the Secret Brother", *The Daily*

never visited Holworth House and a viewing of an exercise for the D-Day invasions did not take place there (as has sometimes been alleged), but much further east at a naval installation near Swanage.

Jack died in 1947 and the house was sold by his family to the current occupants, David and his wife, Helen, who is a church warden at St Catherine's and was, until her recent retirement, headteacher at Crossways Primary School. Helen was on the appointment committee for the new rector. David is a civil engineer who works in Weymouth. He said that they loved living in Holworth House which has a privileged site, one of the "most fantastic" in southern England with wonderful views of the coast and a private beach under the cliff. There are eight bedrooms and three acres of land. The upkeep of the house is almost a full-time job in itself. They mend the roof and draw the wood, but close off part of the house in winter to save energy costs. The house was built with walls one metre thick to withstand the gales. All around are the remains of radar poles from a system established at Ringstead during the war.

Cliff House

Kristine and Paul moved to Cliff House from the Warmwell Estate with small children about thirteen years ago. The family lived originally at the Jacobean manor house at Warmwell. It had been purchased in 1945 by Paul's grandfather, a mining engineer in South Africa, with funds

---

Telegraph, 31 October, 2007,
http://www.telegraph.co.uk/expat/?xml=/global/2007/10/31/noindex/ftchurchill131.xml

St. Catherine's Church

View from the Churchyard

from the sale of Stockwell Park in Bedfordshire, which had belonged to his wife's family and was the subject of compulsory purchase for the development of Luton and the building of the M1.

Paul buys and sells rural properties and manages his investments. Kristine, who is of Danish origin, is a designer and has made the interior of Cliff House very Scandinavian in style. She does yoga and meditation classes at the house. They both love the isolation and spectacular beauty of Cliff House, calling attention to its remoteness, though they said it was never dull living so close to nature and the ever-changing weather. They felt that it was "as if one lived in infinity", making it rather uncomfortable to return to built-up, crowded places. They both felt that it was inspiring and were particularly attached to the isolated footpaths which go in either direction from the house.

Kristine spent the best part of ten years getting the garden in order with a limited number of robust plants such as lavender and santolina, both low and compact and therefore suitable to such an exposed location. Together with the hedges surrounding the house they seem to undulate down the cliff as if they were sculpted. The garden has been featured in *Coast Magazine* and *Gardens Illustrated*.

Rose Cottage

Jane and Neville, who also have a family association with the Warmwell estate, share Rose Cottage with Jane's brother and several other family members. Jane's mother built Cliff House. The cottage had belonged to Harry Miller who was a local lobster fisherman. Her family used to camp in the grounds. When Harry died, her family bought the cottage and the land around it. They feel passionate about the place and have held receptions for two family weddings and a christening in the grounds, following services at St Catherine's. Although they only spend summer holidays at Rose Cottage, they said that its image and location are always in their thoughts. Jane has a painting of the view in her home in London. It is very rustic: they have changed almost nothing since they bought it in the 1950s.

Helwarden House

The name of the house is one of the several ancient names of Holworth. It was constructed from three cottages next to a spring in about 1780. Richard's family lived in Hampstead and bought the house in the 1930s as a holiday home. He had many reminiscences of spending part of the war there. A stone wall separated them from the exclusion zone taken over by the army in the area surrounding Portland and Weymouth from which local residents were evacuated.

Richard studied naval architecture on the Clyde, in Devon and in Sweden. He works in Poole and is a very keen yachtsman. During the war no pleasure boats were allowed along the coast. He built a dinghy and waited for the end of hostilities. Later he built three larger cruisers in the garden – limited to 33ft – the dimensions of the perimeter wall. He enjoys racing and has done many Fastnet races. Julia is a very accomplished painter and does sketches of the coastline when they are out sailing. The prints of her work sell in a gallery in Swanage.

Mirran

Peter and Wendy have lived in Mirran for twelve years. They bought the house in a very dilapidated state and spend five years transforming it, doubling its size. They had previously lived in Hampshire. Wendy is a landscape designer and Peter is retired. He had previously worked as a graphic designer. They started a B&B some years ago and the business now seems to be taking off. Peter participated in the design stage of the refurbishment of St Catherine's church and Wendy does the flowers for the services.

View from Holworth House

Epilogue

The village in the early winter of 2014

In the dead of winter, there are early daffodils at the entrance to the village on the main road and in front of the church. On 6 January, 2014, I gave the first talk of the year to the Monday Club, "Owermoigne from the Earliest Times". The coast and the river valleys were being pounded with winter tides and floods, but the village seemed snug on its high ground. The fields were very wet, though, which was making things difficult for the farmers.

I thought people would be interested in the Celtic origins of the name of the village which had in recent years been a lively controversy among linguists. About forty people attended, mostly the older people from the village, the usual members of the Monday Club. A few fell asleep in the warm comfort of the hall on a cold afternoon. But there were lively questions at the end about old maps and locations, about button-making in the nineteenth century and smuggling.

The previous September the parish had celebrated the new church roof, using the old tiles, carefully replaced one by one by a local firm once the rotted wooden joists had been renewed. There was an open house which included a display of the church records from 1569 brought to the village from the county archives by Jean Coates, the rector, who retired the following month. The records were placed in the chancel on pew cushions. They were avidly scrutinised by many people looking over the lists of baptisms, marriages and funerals for ancient family names.

The weather was beautiful that September day and coffee and tea were served in a tent in the garden. People admired the flowers in the church arranged by the customary team, the wild garden near the old gravestones and "God's pocket", the quiet enclosed area for peace and contemplation in a woodland setting. Geoff had proudly replaced the small sundial over the entry porch which he had carefully cleaned from 150 years of grime and weather. It still worked. As the person mainly responsible for all the fund raising of £50,000, he was justly proud.

Bob, the chair of the village hall, decided to retire after ten years of active building and refurbishment of the prewar structure which had been decidedly rickety and in need of attention when he took over. Funds had been raised from many sources, including the Heritage Lottery Fund, matched by local funds raised from activities in the village hall and the thriving Saturday market held on the first Saturday of every month. Among the current activities are exercise and Pilates classes, bowls, table tennis, dog training, bingo, skittles, clubs and coffee mornings. The twice monthly coffee mornings with bacon rolls have remained a regular feature, giving neighbours an opportunity to meet, and are especially appreciated by some of the oldest people in the village who attend thanks to lifts from family or neighbours. It gives people an opportunity to have village news and find out about forthcoming activities.

After more than twenty-five years, a new Owermoigne youth club was announced by Jill, one of the church wardens. The purpose is to try to improve church attendance. The initial meeting was a craft session for making decorated candles in the village hall, as it was in the weeks leading up to Christmas. Looking for suggestions, Jill proposed a beach clean, a village clean and celebrations for church festivals throughout the year. She asked for further suggestions. There were further meetings and the activity has morphed into a new Sunday school at the church after a gap of ten years. Sandra took a break from her growing online knitted wig enterprise to suggest "Let's dance!" in the parish magazine, a monthly get together for all ages with music from her iTunes list.

The selection of the new rector was underway. Contrary to earlier reports about the landed gentry taking a very large role, there are in fact two representatives from each of the benefice parishes who will serve on the selection panel. For Owermoigne, it is Martin Cree, the owner of Moignes Court and Helen Boyce, the retired headteacher of Crossways School who lives in Holworth House. Interviews took place in March. Interim prayer meetings were sometimes held at Dulcie's house, as she has become too elderly to attend services. Curate, Anthony Bush, and deacon, Jenny Bagnall from West Knighton, seem able to manage all the benefice services. A new rector has been appointed and will hold his first service in June. Of the three candidates, he was the youngest, arriving from a curacy in Devon.

The parish council meeting in January included a heated exchange between local councillors and the county and district councillors in attendance about the local bus service. It has been reduced to once weekly on a Wednesday and an irate woman attended to say that the newly installed digital sign in the bus shelter on the main road indicated that very morning that the 103 was on time. But after waiting in the pouring rain and wind in the shelter, she retreated to a neighbour to phone only to see the bus sail by without stopping! There were angry comments from the parish councillors to the county representative about this poor service, mentioning the hardship for the few people who do not have cars or those who are too old to drive. While the parish council has fought hard to retain a more regular service, it seems as impossible as elsewhere in outlying rural areas.

Together with complaints about potholes in the roads and maintenance of the grass verges and hedges, the cuts in county services delivery were deplored, a sad resonance of similar problems in other rural areas. The launch of a new position, a countryside ranger, was greeted by derision by several village councillors in view of the stringent policies and poor service provision. There was some discussion about the possibility of the construction of more affordable homes on the edge of the village. There was a question about the lack of services – no local school, no shop, and now almost no transport. A letter from a county civil servant, proposing the new scheme, suggested that having more local residents might promote an upgrade of the village and therefore a reassessment of services. This was greeted with further grunts of disapproval. Only four people from the village attended which is customary, unless there is something controversial on the agenda.

No crime was reported. There was notification that Winfrith, the former nuclear reactor site which continued to function after the decommissioning of the reactor in the 1970s as an independent research and commercial site, will finally be demolished. That would be no harm to the environment as it is a large bright turquoise building visible from all over Tadnoll Heath, which is maintained by the Dorset Wildlife Trust. But it signalled the end of an era when incomers in the 1960s brought new life to village activities in Wool, Owermoigne, Broadmayne and other local villages.

There is an heir for Moignes Court and the estate, born in late December. In January, four generations of the family gathered for photos, including Pam at 90, the great grandmother and the new father, Ralph. Martin Cree had grown a beard in order to portray his grandfather, Alfred Pope, the prominent Dorchester brewery owner, in a play. Written by the playwright Rupert Creed for the community theatre group, it is called "Drummer Hodge", based on a poem of Thomas Hardy by the same name, about a young man from the area who was killed in the Boer War. Written in 1899, it was a decidedly anti-war poem which is the core story, but it also includes events of the time in Dorset including the campaign for women's suffrage.

At a coffee morning in the village hall in February, newly equipped with a coffee machine which makes latte and cappuccino, the talk was all about the spring bulbs beginning to show their heads. The recent months of rain and wind in the South West which turned Chesil Beach back to its former shape of 300 years ago and battered the coastline did not affect the village, as it is not on or near the coast or a river. There was though an eighteen-hour power cut in late January. Derek said several couples scurried throughout the village to bring hot food, camping stoves and candles to most of the older people who were on their own. It was wonderful he said, "just like the wartime spirit I remember."

Made in the USA
Charleston, SC
21 August 2015